Classic
ORIENTAL DISHES

Classic
ORIENTAL DISHES

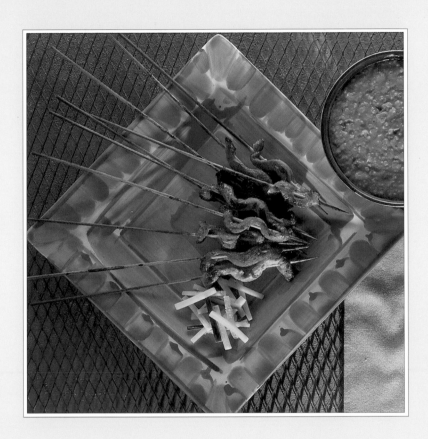

Sue Ashworth • Carol Bowen • Carole Handslip • Kathryn Hawkins
Cara Hobday • Deh-Ta Hsiung • Wendy Lee • Rosemary Wadey

·PARRAGON·

First published in Great Britain in 1996 by
Parragon Book Service Ltd
Unit 13–17
Avonbridge Trading Estate
Atlantic Road
Avonmouth
Bristol BS11 9QD

ISBN: 0-7525-1612-4

Printed in Italy

Produced by Haldane Mason, London

Acknowledgements
Editor: Lisa Dyer
Design: Digital Artworks Partnership Ltd
Photography: Karl Adamson, Sue Atkinson, Iain Bagwell, Martin Brigdale,
Amanda Heywood, Joff Lee, Clive Streeter
Home Economists: Sue Ashworth, Joanna Craig, Jill Eggleton, Carole Handslip,
Kathryn Hawkins, Cara Hobday, Deh-Ta Hsiung, Wendy Lee, Rosemary Wadey

Material in this book has previously appeared in *Barbecues, Chinese Cantonese Cooking,
Chinese Szechuan Cooking, Low-Fat Cooking, Quick & Easy Meals, Thai Cooking,
Vegetarian Chinese Cooking, Vegetarian Dinner Parties, Vegetarian Thai Cooking*
and *Wok Cooking.*

Note
Cup measurements in this book are for American cups.
Tablespoons are assumed to be 15ml. Unless otherwise stated, milk is assumed to be full-
fat, eggs are standard size 2 and pepper is freshly ground black pepper.

CONTENTS

INTRODUCTION

The culinary delights of the Orient are explored in this cookbook, bringing together recipes from China, Japan and South-east Asia. Many of the dishes from these different countries use similar ingredients, and fish and rice are staples. Generally, the food from these regions takes much longer to prepare than to cook, but much of the preparation can be done in advance.

China is a vast country, and its food products and climate are similarly varied. Each region has a distinctive style of cooking, from Peking in the north to Canton in the south, and Shanghi in the east to Szechuan in the west, but all emphasize the harmonious blending of colour, aroma, flavour and texture in a single dish or course of dishes. Szechuan food is noted for being hot, spicy and strongly flavoured. Chillies are used in large quantities, and garlic, onions and spring onions are also basic ingredients. Aromatic ground rice and sesame seeds are often used to coat meat, and sesame paste is the principal ingredient in sauces. Beef is the most popular meat, and this region is known for its meat preservation techniques, such as salting, drying, smoking and pickling. Yunnan in the deep south-west is an even more remote region than Szechuan and its best-known product is ham, although it is also known for rabbit and venison dishes.

The crispy Peking duck, prepared with hoisin sauce, is the speciality of Peking cuisine, but pork and noodle dishes are also favourites. Standard Cantonese dishes include many recipes that are popular with Westerners, such as egg rolls, egg foo yung and pork dishes. Fish, prawns (shrimp), minced chicken and tofu (bean curd) are basic ingredients in the cooking of the Shanghai region, and shredded fish and meat are typical of the Fukien region. Although famous for its sushi and sashimi, Japan offers many other culinary pleasures, such as tempura (deep fried fish or vegetables), sukiyaki and teriyaki dishes, and miso soups.

Indonesia consists of many small islands, and the Chinese, Dutch and Portuguese have influenced the cuisine of this area. Nasi goreng, a fried rice dish, and gado gado, a salad of vegetables served with a spicy peanut sauce, are served throughout Malaysia and the islands. Thai food is often described as having a greater complexity of flavours and textures than Indonesian or Malay food, although they all rely on the same basic ingredients for cooking. Thailand has a highly unique cuisine that has changed little over the centuries, despite regular foreign intervention. Although the influence of China and India can be seen in the stir-fries and curries, these dishes are adapted by the use of herbs, spices and coconut milk. The use of galangal, lemon grass, lime and fish sauce gives Thai food its characteristic flavour.

COOKING METHODS AND EQUIPMENT

The equipment needed for cooking oriental dishes is readily available to Western cooks.
A wok is useful for more than stir-frying: it can be used for braising, deep-frying, steaming, boiling,
poaching and even making soups. There are two types available: the traditional iron version and the
modern non-stick version. The traditional wok is extremely reasonable in price but it must be
'seasoned' first by rubbing oil on to the iron, heating the wok, then rubbing off the excess oil. The
modern version gives perfectly good results and is easier to clean. However, you will not be able to use
metal utensils with these; instead use wooden spoons, chopsticks or spatulas. Many woks are sold
complete with these utensils, including a handy rice paddle.
A good all-purpose meat cleaver for slicing, shredding, peeling, crushing and chopping
is useful, but try out different weights so you find one that suits you. Ladles, spatulas and chopsticks
are useful for transferring ingredients and stirring. Traditional bamboo steamers that stack on top of
each other are useful, but the wok can be used on its own as a steamer with a rack or trivet inside and
the dome-shaped wok lid on top. It is worth investing in a rice cooker only if you are seriously keen on
oriental foods and eat large quantities of rice. Having said that, most Asian homes have two
or maybe three rice cookers of different sizes and would be lost without one.

SPECIAL INGREDIENTS

Many of these ingredients can be found in supermarkets. The more specialist items, such as
fish sauce, black bean sauce or Kaffir lime leaves, can be found in oriental shops or markets.

Baby sweetcorn Baby corn cobs have a wonderfully sweet fragrance and flavour, and an irresistible texture. They are available both fresh and canned.

Bamboo shoots Still only available canned and sometimes dried (which need soaking before use), bamboo shoots are the crunchy cream-coloured shoots of the bamboo plant.

Banana leaves These are the large green, inedible leaves of the banana tree that are principally used in Malay and Thai cooking for wrapping food and for making containers for steaming purposes. They give the food a slightly aromatic, delicate flavour, but cannot be eaten.

Basil Holy basil, or Thai basil, available from specialist stores, has a stronger, more pungent and sharper flavour than the European sweet basil. When unavailable, use ordinary basil in the same proportions.

Bean sauce A thick sauce made from yellow or black soya beans. The crushed beans are mixed with flour, vinegar, spices and salt to make a spicy, sometimes salty, and definitely aromatic sauce. It is usually sold in cans or jars.

Bean-sprouts These tiny, crunchy shoots of mung or soya beans are widely available fresh and should be used on the day of purchase. Canned bean-sprouts are available but generally lack flavour and crunchiness.

Black bean sauce Sold in jars or cans, this sauce is made from salted beans that have been crushed and mixed with flour and spices (such as ginger, garlic or chilli) to make a thickish paste. Once opened, keep in the refrigerator.

Chilli bean sauce This is fermented bean paste mixed with hot chillies and seasonings. Some sauces are quite mild, but others are very hot. You will have to try out various brands to see which one is to your taste.

Chilli paste This is a paste of roast ground chillies mixed with oil. Depending upon the chillies used, the colour and flavour will differ appreciably, so only add a small amount to err on the side of safety. It is sold in small jars and may be called 'ground chillies in oil'. A small jar will last a long time if stored in the refrigerator.

Chilli sauce A very hot sauce made from chillies, vinegar, sugar and salt. Usually sold in bottles, the sauce should be used sparingly in cooking or as a dip. Tabasco sauce can be a substitute.

Chillies Fresh chillies come in varying degrees of hotness. Cooking helps to mellow the flavour, but a degree of caution should be exercised when using them. If you do not like your food too hot, then discard the seeds when you prepare the chillies. Remember at all costs to make sure you wash your hands thoroughly after touching them as they contain an irritant which will burn the eyes and mouth on contact. Fresh chopped hot chillies can be replaced with chilli paste or powder, but the result will be a little different. As a general guide for buying, the smaller the chilli, the hotter it will be. Thai chillies are small and very hot, but the larger types are often stocked in most supermarkets and these are perhaps the best to use when in any doubt.
Dried chillies add a good kick to a dish, especially if they are tossed in oil with other spices at the beginning of cooking.

Generally, the chillies are added whole, but they can sometimes be halved. In most cases these should be removed from the dish before serving. Again, the smaller the dried chilli, the hotter the flavour.

Chinese leaves Also known as Chinese cabbage, there are two widely available varieties. The most commonly seen one is a pale green colour and has a tightly wrapped, elongated head – about two-thirds of the cabbage is stem which has a crunchy texture. The other variety has a shorter, fatter head with curlier, pale yellow or green leaves, also with white stems.

Coconut The coconut is used in many Thai and Malay dishes, both sweet and savoury, and is infinitely better to use than desiccated (shredded) coconut. Many supermarkets now stock them fresh at little cost.

Coconut milk Coconut milk is an infusion used to flavour and thicken many South-east Asian dishes. Perhaps the best and easiest type to use comes in cans from oriental shops, but remember to check that it is unsweetened for savoury dishes.

Coriander (Cilantro) This is a delicate and fragrant herb, also known as cilantro or Chinese parsley. The roots have a more intense flavour and are generally used for cooking, while the leaves are used more for flavouring the cooked and finished dish. Chopped leaves are frequently stirred into a cooked dish or scattered over the surface just before serving.

Curry leaves Rather like bay leaves, but not quite so thick and luscious, these are highly aromatic leaves that are chopped, torn or left whole and added to many curries and slow-simmering dishes. Olive-green in colour, they can be bought fresh or dried from specialist shops.

Fish paste This thick paste is made from fermented fish or shrimps and salt. It is used only in small amounts since it has enormous flavouring power. Anchovy paste makes a good, if not authentic, alternative.

Fish sauce Known by the name of nam pla or nuoc nam, this salty, thin brown sauce is widely used in South-east Asian cooking instead of salt. It is made by pressing salted fish and is available in many oriental food shops. There is really no good substitute, so the sauce is worthy hunting for.

Five-spice powder A mixture of star anise, fennel seeds, cloves, cinnamon bark and Szechuan pepper. It is very pungent, so should be used sparingly. It will keep indefinitely in an airtight container.

Galangal Very similar to ginger, galangal is a root that can be bought fresh from oriental food shops, but it is also available dried and as a powder. The fresh root needs to be peeled before slicing, while dried pieces need to be soaked in water before using and then discarded from the dish before serving. If fresh galangal is unavailable for a recipe, then substitute 1 dried slice or 1 teaspoon of powder for each 1.5 cm/½ inch piece of fresh.

Ginger Always peel ginger root before using, then chop, grate or blend to a paste to use. Buy it in small quantities to ensure freshness and store in a plastic bag in the refrigerator. Dried ginger powder is no substitute.

Hoisin sauce Also known as barbecue sauce, this is made from soya beans, sugar, vinegar, salt, garlic, chilli and sesame oil. Sold in cans or jars, it will keep in the refrigerator for several months.

Kaffir lime leaves These are dark green, glossy leaves that have a lemony-lime flavour which can be bought from special shops, either fresh or dried. Fresh leaves impart the most delicious flavour to a dish, so are worth seeking out. Many Thai recipes call for Kaffir lime leaves and they can be shredded with a pair of scissors or left whole. When stocks cannot be found, substitute a leaf with about 1 teaspoon of finely grated lemon rind.

Lemon grass Also known as citronelle, lemon grass is a tropical grass with a pungent, aromatic lemon flavour. It is fairly easy to buy fresh from supermarkets. When chopped lemon grass is specified, use the thick bulky end of the spring onion-like (scallion-like) stem. Alternatively, if the whole stem is required, beat well to bruise so the flavour can be imparted. Stalks keep well in the refrigerator for up to about 2 weeks. When unavailable, use grated lemon rind. Dried lemon grass is also available as a powder called sereh.

Noodles There are many types available, and although some are interchangeable, it is best to use those which a recipe calls for. Choose from rice noodles or sticks, medium–flat rice noodles, rice vermicelli or very thin rice noodles, egg noodles and 'cellophane' or very thin transparent noodles. Dried noodles need to be soaked in cold water before using, during which time they double their weight. They then require only a very short cooking time. Fresh noodles do not require any precooking and they are cooked in the same way as the presoaked dried variety.

Oyster sauce Oriental oyster sauce, a light sauce made from oysters and soy sauce, is frequently used in Chinese, Japanese and Thai dishes. It is used to flavour meat and vegetables during cooking. Despite it's name it is entirely free from the flavour of oysters, or indeed of fish.

Palm sugar This thick, coarse brown sugar has a slightly caramel taste. It is sold in round cakes or in small, round, flat containers. It is not strictly necessary for most recipes and can usually be replaced with dark, soft brown sugar or demerara sugar.

Plum sauce This is a sweet and sour sauce with a unique fruity flavour. It is best known as a condiment for crispy Peking duck.

Rice Long-grain rice or jasmine rice are the most practical types of rice to serve with oriental dishes. Jasmine rice, also known as Thai fragrant rice, becomes slightly sticky with cooking. Short-grain glutinous rice, which is also known as sticky or waxy rice and is available in Japanese, Chinese and Thai types, is the traditional oriental rice, and it is easy to eat with chopsticks.

Rice vinegar This vinegar is made from rice, but has a far less acidic flavour than Western varieties. There are two basic types: red and white. Red vinegar is made from fermented rice and has a distinctive dark colour and depth of flavour. White vinegar is stronger in flavour as it is distilled from rice wine.

Rice wine Chinese rice wine, made from glutinous rice, is also known as 'yellow wine' (Huang jiu in Chinese), because of its golden amber colour. A good dry or medium sherry can be an acceptable substitute.

Sesame oil This nutty-flavoured oil is generally used in small quantities at the end of cooking for adding flavour. Sometimes sesame oil is used with groundnut (peanut) or sunflower oil for stir-frying.

Shiitake mushrooms Highly fragrant dried mushrooms add a special flavour to dishes. The shiitake is the best known and used in many Chinese dishes. They are not cheap, but a small amount will go a long way and they will keep indefinitely in an airtight jar. Soak them in warm water for 20–30 minutes (or in cold water for several hours), squeeze dry and discard the hard stalks before use.

Shrimp, dried These are strongly flavoured dried prawns (shrimp) available whole or in powder form. Whole ones should be rinsed before use.

Shrimp paste A dark brown, dry paste made from prawns and salt, this paste is used in small amounts to flavour sauces. Anchovy paste makes a good substitute.

Soy sauce Choose from light and dark types. The light variety, hard to find, is light in colour but saltier in taste and still full of flavour. It is the best type to use in cooking. The dark variety is often a little thicker than the light type and more often used as a condiment or dipping sauce.

Star anise A Chinese spice with distinctive liquorice flavour. It is a spice that is shaped like a star with eight points, and it is used to flavour meat and poultry dishes in particular.

Stock Fresh stocks are essential for stir-frying, braising and making soups. Many supermarkets carry fresh fish and chicken stocks, but the best ones are those you make at home. For an oriental-flavoured stock, try the recipe, right.

Straw mushrooms Grown on beds of rice straw, hence the name, straw mushrooms have a pleasant slippery texture and a subtle taste. Canned straw mushrooms should be rinsed and drained after opening.

Szechuan peppercorns Also known as fa-jui, these are wild reddish-brown peppercorns from Szechuan. More aromatic but less hot than either white or black peppercorns, they do give a unique flavour to food.

Tofu Also called bean curd, this a food made from puréed and pressed soya beans. Sold in flat cakes, it has the texture and consistency of soft cheese. Available plain and bland or smoked, it is highly nutritious and does take on the flavour of the other ingredients it is being cooked with. The type used for stir-frying should be firm so that it does not crumble during cooking, and is best cut into cubes for use. Don't be tempted to over-mix or stir too vigorously during preparation. It makes a very good ingredient for sweet and savoury dishes and is ideal for vegetarian dishes.

Water chestnuts Also known as horse's hooves in China because of their appearance before the skin is peeled off, these give a lovely crunch to a stir-fry, salad or vegetable accompaniment.

Wonton skins These are thin, yellow discs of dough generally packed in cellophane for easy use. Store in the refrigerator before use. Do not allow them to dry out, or they will become dry, brittle and unsuitable for wrapping around sweet and savoury mixtures that are steamed or fried. Filo pastry makes a good alternative when wonton skins are unavailable.

Wood ears Also known as cloud ears, this is a dried black fungus sold in oriental stores. It should be soaked in cold or warm water for 20 minutes, then rinsed in fresh water before use. It has a crunchy texture and a mild flavour.

Yellow bean sauce A thick paste made from salted, fermented yellow soya beans, crushed with flour and sugar. It is sold in cans or jars, and once the can is opened, the sauce should be transferred to a screw-top jar. It will then keep for months in the refrigerator.

Chinese Stock

Makes 2.5 litres/4 pints/10 cups
750 g/1½ lb chicken pieces, trimmed and chopped
750 g/1½ lb pork spare ribs, trimmed and chopped
3.75 litres/6 pints/15 cups cold water
3–4 pieces ginger root, crushed
3–4 spring onions (scallions), roughly chopped
3–4 tbsp Chinese rice wine or dry sherry

Place the chicken and pork in a large saucepan with the water. Add the ginger and spring onions (scallions). Bring to the boil and skim the scum off the the top. Reduce the heat and simmer uncovered for at least 2–3 hours.
Strain the stock, discarding the chicken, pork, ginger and spring onions (scallions). Add the rice wine or sherry, return to the boil and simmer for 2–3 minutes. Refrigerate the stock when cool. It will keep for 4–5 days.

APPETIZERS & SOUPS

A number of dishes can be served as an appetizer before a meal – just like hors-d'oeuvres in the West. Instead of serving different appetizers individually, try serving a small portion of each together as an assorted hors-d'oeuvre, in a similar way to dim sum. Select three or four different items each. Remember not to have more than one of the same type of food, and the recipes should be chosen for their harmony and balance in colour, flavour and texture. Try a selection of Crispy Vegetarian Spring Rolls, Money Bags and Butterfly Prawns (Shrimp), for example, or choose a soup to serve as a starter if you prefer. There is a good selection of soups from which to choose on the following pages, from the Thai-style Chicken & Coconut Soup to Chinese Wonton Soup.

CRUDITES WITH SHRIMP SAUCE (PAGE 14)

CRISPY SEAWEED

Popular in many Chinese restaurants, this dish is served as a starter before a main meal. This 'seaweed' is in fact deep-fried spring greens.

SERVES 4

INGREDIENTS:
250 g/8 oz spring greens
vegetable oil, for deep-frying
1½ tsp caster (superfine) sugar
1 tsp salt
30 g/1 oz/¼ cup flaked (slivered) almonds

1 Wash the spring greens thoroughly. Trim off the excess tough stalks. Place on paper towels or a dry tea towel (dish cloth) and leave to drain.

2 ▲ Using a sharp knife, finely shred the spring greens and spread them out on paper towels for about 30 minutes to dry.

3 ▲ Heat the oil in a wok or deep-fat fryer. Remove the pan from the heat and add the spring greens in batches.

Return the pan to the heat and deep-fry until the greens begin to float to the surface and become translucent and crinkled. Remove the spring greens, using a perforated spoon, and drain on paper towels. Keep each batch warm.

4 ▼ Mix the sugar and salt together, sprinkle over the 'seaweed' and toss together to mix well.

5 ▼ Add the flaked (slivered) almonds to the hot oil and fry until lightly golden. Remove with a perforated spoon and drain on paper towels.

6 Serve the crispy 'seaweed' with the flaked (slivered) almonds

SWEET & SOUR CUCUMBER

Chunks of cucumber are marinated in vinegar and sweetened with honey to make a sweet and sour appetizer.

SERVES 4

INGREDIENTS:
1 cucumber
1 tsp salt
2 tsp honey
2 tbsp rice vinegar
*3 tbsp chopped fresh coriander
   (cilantro)*
2 tsp sesame oil
‡ tsp crushed red peppercorns
*strips of red and yellow (bell) pepper, to
   garnish*

1 ▼ Peel thin strips off the cucumber along the length. Cut the cucumber in quarters lengthways and then into 2.5 cm/1 inch long pieces. Place in a colander.

2 ▼ Sprinkle the salt over the cucumber and leave to rest for 30 minutes to allow the salt to draw out the excess water from the cucumber.

3 Rinse the cucumber well to remove the salt and pat dry with paper towels.

4 ▼ Place the cucumber in a bowl. Combine the honey with the vinegar and pour over. Mix together and leave to marinate for 15 minutes.

5 ▼ Stir the coriander (cilantro) and sesame oil into the cucumbers, then transfer to a serving bowl.

6 Sprinkle over the crushed red peppercorns. Serve garnishished with strips of red and yellow (bell) pepper.

CRUDITES WITH SHRIMP SAUCE

This is a classic Thai starter – fruit and vegetable crudités served with a spicy, garlicky shrimp sauce. It is served at every meal, and each family has their own favourite recipe. Hard-boiled (hard-cooked) quails' eggs are a traditional addition to this platter and you may like to include some.

SERVES 6

INGREDIENTS:
about 750 g/1½ lb prepared raw fruit and vegetables, such as broccoli, cauliflower, apple, pineapple, cucumber, celery, (bell) peppers and mushrooms

SHRIMP SAUCE:
60 g/2 oz dried shrimps
1 cm/½ inch cube shrimp paste
3 garlic cloves, crushed
4 red chillies, deseeded and chopped
6 stems fresh coriander (cilantro), coarsely chopped
3 tbsp lime juice
Thai fish sauce, to taste
brown sugar, to taste

1 To make the sauce, first soak the dried shrimps in warm water for 10 minutes.

2 ▼ Then place the shrimp paste, drained soaked shrimps, garlic, chillies and coriander (cilantro) in a food processor or blender and process until well chopped but not smooth.

3 ▲ Turn the sauce mixture into a bowl and add the lime juice, mixing well.

4 ▲ Add fish sauce and brown sugar to taste to the sauce, mixing to blend well. Cover the bowl tightly and chill the sauce in the refrigerator for at least 12 hours, or overnight.

5 To serve, arrange the fruit and vegetables attractively on a large serving plate. Place the prepared sauce in the centre for dipping.

CRISPY VEGETARIAN SPRING ROLLS

This recipe uses a cornflour (cornstarch) paste. To make the paste, mix 1 part cornflour (cornstarch) with about 1½ parts cold water until smooth. For a non-vegetarian version of these spring rolls, just replace mushrooms with chicken or pork, and the carrots with prawns (shrimps).

MAKES 12 ROLLS

INGREDIENTS:
125 g/4 oz fresh bean-sprouts, washed and drained
60 g/2 oz spring onions (scallions)
60 g/2 oz carrots
60 g/2 oz canned sliced bamboo shoots, rinsed and drained
60 g/2 oz mushrooms
2-3 tbsp vegetable oil, plus oil, for deep-frying
½ tsp salt
½ tsp sugar
1 tbsp light soy sauce
1 tsp Chinese rice wine or dry sherry
12 spring roll skins, defrosted if frozen
1 tbsp cornflour (cornstarch) paste
flour, for dusting
vegetable oil, for deep-frying

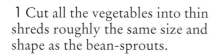

1 Cut all the vegetables into thin shreds roughly the same size and shape as the bean-sprouts.

2 Heat the oil in a hot wok and stir-fry the vegetables for about 1 minute. Add the salt, sugar, soy sauce and wine and continue stirring for 1½–2 minutes. Remove the vegetables from the wok with a slotted spoon and place in a bowl. Drain off the excess liquid, then leave to cool.

3 ▼ To make the spring rolls, place about 2 tablespoons of the vegetables one-third of the way down on a spring roll skin, with the triangle pointing away from you.

4 ▼ Lift the lower flap over the filling and fold in one end.

5 ▼ Roll once and fold in the other end.

6 Roll once more, brush the upper edge with a little cornflour (cornstarch) paste, and roll into a neat package. Lightly dust a tray with flour and place the spring roll with the flap-side down. Make the rest of the spring rolls in the same way.

7 Heat the oil in a wok or deep-fryer until smoking, then reduce the heat to low and deep-fry the spring rolls in batches for 2–3 minutes or until golden and crispy. Remove with a slotted spoon and drain on paper towels. Serve hot with a dip sauce such as soy sauce, sweet and sour sauce or chilli sauce.

RICE CUBES WITH DIPPING SAUCE

Plain rice cubes are a good foil to any piquant dipping sauce, and they are often served with satay to complement the dipping sauce. Basmati rice could be substituted for the jasmine rice, but avoid using any rice labelled 'easy cook' or 'par-boiled'.

SERVES 4–6

INGREDIENTS:
300 g/10 oz/1½ cups Thai jasmine rice
1.25 litres/2¼ pints/5 cups water

CORIANDER (CILANTRO)
DIPPING SAUCE:
1 garlic clove
2 tsp salt
1 tbsp black peppercorns
60 g/2 oz/1 cup washed fresh coriander (cilantro), including roots and stem
3 tbsp lemon juice
180 ml/6 fl oz/¾ cup coconut milk
2 tbsp peanut butter
2 spring onions (scallions), chopped roughly
1 red chilli, deseeded and sliced

1 Grease and line a 20 × 10 × 2.5 cm/ 8 × 4 × 1 inch tin (pan).

2 ▼ To make the sauce, put the garlic, salt, peppercorns, coriander (cilantro) and lemon juice into a pestle and mortar or blender. Grind finely.

3 ▼ Add the coconut milk, peanut butter, spring onions (scallions) and chilli. Grind finely. Transfer to a saucepan and bring to the boil. Leave to cool. This sauce will keep for 3–5 days in a refrigerator.

4 To cook the rice, do not rinse. Bring the water to the boil and add the rice. Stir and return to a medium boil. Cook, uncovered, for 14–16 minutes until very soft. Drain thoroughly.

5 Put 125 g/4 oz/⅔ cup of the cooked rice in a blender and combine, or grind to a paste in a pestle and mortar.

6 ▼ Stir the ground rice into the remaining cooked rice and spoon into the lined tin (pan). Level the surface and cover with clingfilm (plastic wrap). Compress the rice by using either a similar-sized tin (pan) which will fit into the filled tin (pan), or a small piece of board, and weigh this down with cans or kitchen scale weights. Chill for at least 8 hours or preferably overnight.

7 Invert the tin (pan) on to a board. Cut the rice into cubes with a wet knife. Serve with the coriander (cilantro) dipping sauce.

MUSHROOM WONTONS WITH PIQUANT DIPPING SAUCE

Mushroom-filled crispy wontons are served on skewers with a dipping sauce flavoured with chillies.

SERVES 4

INGREDIENTS:
8 wooden skewers
1 tbsp vegetable oil
1 tbsp chopped onion
1 small garlic clove, chopped
¼ tsp chopped ginger root
60 g/2 oz/¼ cup flat mushrooms, chopped
16 wonton skins (see page 29)
vegetable oil, for deep-frying
salt

PIQUANT DIPPING SAUCE:
2 tbsp vegetable oil
2 spring onions (scallions), shredded thinly
1 red and 1 green chilli, deseeded and shredded thinly
3 tbsp light soy sauce
1 tbsp vinegar
1 tbsp dry sherry
pinch of sugar

2 ▲ Place 1 teaspoon of the cooled mushroom filling in the centre of each wonton skin. Bring two opposite corners together to cover the mixture and pinch together to seal. Repeat with the remaining corners.

3 Thread 2 wontons on to each skewer. Heat enough oil in a large saucepan to deep-fry the wontons in batches until golden and crisp. Remove with a perforated spoon and drain on paper towels.

4 To make the sauce, first heat the oil in a small saucepan until quite hot. To test the oil, drop a small cube of bread in the oil; if it browns in a few seconds the oil is the correct temperature.

5 ▲ Put the shredded spring onions (scallions) and chillies in a bowl and pour the hot oil slowly on top. Then stir in the remaining sauce ingredients, mixing well, and serve with the crispy mushroom wontons.

1 ▲ Heat the oil in a wok or frying pan (skillet). Add the onion, garlic and ginger root and stir-fry for 2 minutes. Stir in the mushrooms and fry for a further 2 minutes. Season well with salt and leave to cool.

CRISPY-FRIED VEGETABLES WITH HOT & SWEET DIPPING SAUCE

A Thai-style sauce makes the perfect accompaniment to fried vegetables.

SERVES 4

INGREDIENTS:
vegetable oil, for deep-frying
500 g/1 lb selection of vegetables, such as cauliflower, broccoli, mushrooms, courgettes (zucchini), (bell) peppers and baby sweetcorn, cut into pieces

BATTER:
125 g/4 oz/1 cup plain (all-purpose) flour
½ tsp salt
1 tsp caster (superfine) sugar
1 tsp baking powder
3 tbsp vegetable oil
200 ml/7 fl oz/scant 1 cup warm water

SAUCE:
6 tbsp light malt vinegar
2 tbsp Thai fish sauce or light soy sauce
2 tbsp water
1 tbsp soft brown sugar
pinch of salt
2 garlic cloves, crushed
2 tsp grated fresh root ginger
2 red chillies, deseeded and chopped
2 tbsp chopped fresh coriander (cilantro)

1 ▼ To make the batter, sift the flour, salt, sugar and baking powder into a large bowl. Add the oil and most of the water. Whisk together to make a smooth batter, adding extra water to give it the consistency of single (light) cream. Chill for 20–30 minutes.

2 ▼ Meanwhile, make the sauce. Heat the vinegar, fish sauce or soy sauce, water, sugar and salt until boiling. Remove from the heat and leave to cool.

3 Mix together the garlic, ginger, chillies and coriander (cilantro) in a small serving bowl. Pour over the cooled vinegar mixture and stir together to combine.

4 ▼ Heat the oil for deep-frying in a wok or deep-fat fryer to about 180–190°C/350–375°F, or until a cube of bread browns in 30 seconds. Dip the prepared vegetables in the batter and fry them, a few at a time, until crisp and golden – about 2 minutes. Drain on paper towels.

5 Serve the vegetables accompanied by the dipping sauce.

BUTTERFLY PRAWNS (SHRIMP)

Use unpeeled, raw king or tiger prawns (shrimp) which are about 7–10 cm (3–4 inches) long.

SERVES 4

INGREDIENTS:
*12 raw tiger prawns (shrimp) in their shells
2 tbsp light soy sauce
1 tbsp Chinese rice wine or dry sherry
1 tbsp cornflour (cornstarch)
2 eggs, lightly beaten
8–10 tbsp breadcrumbs
vegetable oil, for deep-frying
salt and pepper
shredded lettuce leaves, to serve
chopped spring onions (scallions), to garnish*

1 ▲ Shell the prawns (shrimp) but leave the tails on. Devein by making a shallow cut along the back of each prawn, then pull out the black vein.

2 ▼ Split them in half from the underbelly about halfway along, leaving the tails still firmly attached.

3 Mix together the salt, pepper, soy sauce, wine and cornflour (cornstarch) in a bowl, add the prawns (shrimp) and turn to coat. Leave to marinate for 10–15 minutes.

4 ▼ Pick up each prawn (shrimp) by the tail, dip it in the beaten egg, then roll it in the breadcrumbs to coat evenly.

5 Heat the oil in a wok or deep-fat fryer to about 180–190°C/350–375°F, or until a cube of bread browns in 30 seconds. Deep-fry the prawns (shrimp) in batches until golden brown. Remove them with a slotted spoon and drain on paper towels.

6 To serve, arrange the prawns (shrimp) neatly on a bed of lettuce leaves and garnish with spring onions (scallions), either raw or soaked for about 30 seconds in hot oil.

PORK SATAY

This is the classic satay, which can also be made with chicken. Here the slivers of pork make delicate skewers, which will cook quickly.

SERVES 6–8

✿✦✿✦✿✦✿✦✿✦✿✦✿✦✿✦✿✦✿

INGREDIENTS:

36 wooden skewers, soaked in hand-hot water for 20 minutes
1 kg/2 lb pork (chump end or leg steaks)
1 small onion, sliced finely
2 garlic cloves, crushed
1 tsp ground coriander
1 tsp ground cumin
2 red chillies, deseeded and chopped
2.5 cm/1 inch piece ginger, grated
2 tbsp soy sauce
2 tbsp oil
1 tbsp lemon juice
1 tsp dark brown sugar

PEANUT SAUCE:

1 small onion, quartered
3 garlic cloves, crushed
½ tsp ground coriander
½ tsp ground cumin
1 tbsp lemon juice
1 tsp salt
½ red chilli, deseeded and sliced
120 ml/4 fl oz/½ cup coconut milk
250 g/8 oz/1 cup crunchy peanut butter
250 ml/8 fl oz/1 cup water

✿✦✿✦✿✦✿✦✿✦✿✦✿✦✿✦✿✦✿

1 ▼ Cut the pork into thin slivers, about 12 cm/5 inches long and 1 cm/½ inch thick. Put into a non-porous dish.

2 ▲ Combine the onion, garlic, coriander, cumin, chillies, ginger, soy sauce, oil, lemon juice and brown sugar. Pour over the pork, and stir to make sure that it is evenly coated. Leave to marinate for 2–3 hours.

3 Meanwhile, make the peanut sauce. Chop the onion finely by hand or feed it through the feed tube of a food processor. Then add the remaining ingredients in order, except for the water, and combine thoroughly.

4 Transfer the sauce mixture to a saucepan and add the water. Bring to the boil and cook until the desired thickness is reached. Set aside.

5 ▼ Thread the pork slivers on to the soaked skewers in an 'S' shape.

6 Cook over a medium barbecue (grill) or under a preheated hot grill (broiler) for 10 minutes, turning frequently. Serve hot or cold, accompanied by the peanut sauce.

DEEP-FRIED SPARE RIBS

The spare ribs should be chopped into small bite-sized pieces before or after cooking.

SERVES 4

INGREDIENTS:
8–10 finger spare ribs
1 tsp five-spice powder or 1 tbsp mild curry powder
1 tbsp Chinese rice wine or dry sherry
1 egg
2 tbsp flour
vegetable oil, for deep-frying
1 tsp finely shredded spring onions (scallions)
1 tsp finely shredded fresh green or red hot chillies, deseeded
salt and pepper

SPICY SALT AND PEPPER:
1 tbsp salt
1 tsp ground Szechuan peppercorns
1 tsp five-spice powder

1 Mix all the ingredients for the spicy salt and pepper together. Place in a dry frying pan (skillet) and stir-fry for 3–4 minutes over a low heat, stirring constantly. Allow to cool.

2 ▼ Chop the ribs into 3–4 small pieces. Place the ribs in a bowl with salt, pepper, five-spice or curry powder and the wine. Turn to coat the ribs in the spices and leave them to marinate for 1–2 hours.

3 Mix the egg and flour together to make a batter.

4 ▼ Dip the ribs in the batter one by one to coat well.

5 Heat the oil in a preheated wok until smoking and temperature reaches about 180–190°C/350–375°F. Deep-fry the ribs for 4–5 minutes, then remove with a slotted spoon and drain on paper towels.

5 ▼ Reheat the oil over a high heat and deep-fry the ribs once more for another minute. Remove and drain again on paper towels.

6 Pour 1 tablespoon of the hot oil over the spring onions (scallions) and chillies and leave for 30–40 seconds. Garnish the ribs with the shredded spring onions (scallions) and chillies, and serve with the spicy salt and pepper for dipping.

LITTLE GOLDEN PARCELS

These little parcels will draw admiring gasps from your guests, but they are fairly simple to prepare.

MAKES 30

✽✽✽✽✽✽✽✽✽✽✽✽✽✽✽✽✽✽

INGREDIENTS:
1 garlic clove, crushed
1 tsp chopped coriander (cilantro) root
1 tsp pepper
250 g/8 oz/1 cup boiled mashed potato
175 g/6 oz/1 cup water chestnuts,
  chopped finely
1 tsp grated ginger root
2 tbsp ground roast peanuts
2 tsp light soy sauce
½ tsp salt
½ tsp sugar
30 wonton sheets, defrosted
1 tsp cornflour (cornstarch), made into
  a paste with a little water
  (see page 15)
vegetable oil, for deep-frying
fresh chives, to garnish
sweet chilli sauce, to serve

✽✽✽✽✽✽✽✽✽✽✽✽✽✽✽✽✽✽

1 ▼ Combine all the ingredients thoroughly, except the wonton sheets, cornflour (cornstarch) paste and oil.

2 Keeping the remainder of the wonton sheets covered with a damp cloth, lay 4 sheets out on a work surface (counter).

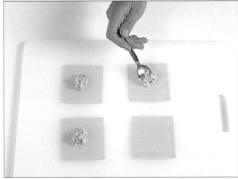

3 ▲ Put a teaspoonful of the mixture on each wonton sheet.

4 ▼ Make a line of the cornflour (cornstarch) paste around each sheet, about 1 cm/½ inch from the edge.

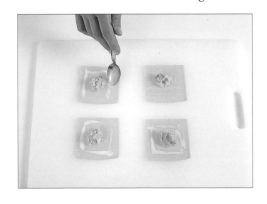

5 ▼ For each sheet, bring all four corners to the centre and press together to form a little bag. Continue the process of filling and wrapping until all the wonton sheets are used.

6 Meanwhile, heat 5 cm/2 inches of the vegetable oil in a deep saucepan until a light haze appears on top and lower the parcels in, in batches of 3. Fry until golden brown, remove with a slotted spoon, and leave to drain on paper towels.

7 Tie a chive around the neck of each bag to garnish, and serve with a sweet chilli sauce for dipping.

MONEY BAGS

These steamed dumplings are made with a mushroom and sweetcorn filling. Eat them as they are, or try dipping them in a mixture of soy sauce, sherry and slivers of ginger root.

SERVES 4

INGREDIENTS:
3 Chinese dried mushrooms (if unavailable, use thinly sliced open-cup mushrooms)
2 tbsp vegetable oil
2 spring onions (scallions), chopped
90 g/3 oz/⅓ cup sweetcorn
½ red chilli, deseeded and chopped
1 tbsp brown bean sauce

WRAPPERS:
250 g/8 oz/2 cups plain (all-purpose) flour
1 egg, beaten
75 ml/3 fl oz/⅓ cup water
1 tsp baking powder
¾ tsp salt

1 Place the dried mushrooms in a small bowl, cover with warm water and leave to soak for 20–25 minutes.

2 ▼ Meanwhile make the wrappers. Sift the flour into a bowl, add the egg and mix in lightly. Stir in the water, baking powder and salt. Mix to make a soft dough. Knead lightly until smooth on a floured board. Cover with a damp cloth and set aside for 5–6 minutes. This allows the baking powder time to activate, so that the dumplings swell when steaming.

3 Drain the soaked mushrooms, squeezing them dry. Remove the tough centres and chop the mushrooms.

4 Heat the vegetable oil in a wok or large frying pan (skillet) and stir-fry the mushrooms, spring onions (scallions), sweetcorn and chilli for about 2 minutes. Stir in the brown bean sauce to coat and remove from the heat.

5 ▼ Roll the dough into a large sausage and cut into 24 even-sized pieces. Roll each piece out into a thin round and place a teaspoonful of the mushroom and sweetcorn filling in the centre.

6 ▼ Gather up the edges to a point, pinch together and twist to seal.

7 ▼ Stand the dumplings in an oiled steaming basket. Place over a saucepan of simmering water, cover and steam for 12–14 minutes before serving.

NOODLE, MUSHROOM & GINGER SOUP

Thai soups are very quickly and easily put together, and are cooked so that each ingredient can still be tasted, even after it has been combined with several others.

SERVES 4

INGREDIENTS:
15 g/½ oz/¼ cup dried Chinese mushrooms or 125 g/4 oz/1½ cups field or chestnut (crimini) mushrooms
1 litre/1¾ pints/4 cups hot vegetable stock
125 g/4 oz thread egg noodles
2 tsp sunflower oil
3 garlic cloves, crushed
2.5 cm/1 inch piece ginger, shredded finely
½ tsp mushroom ketchup
1 tsp light soy sauce
125 g/4 oz/2 cups bean-sprouts
coriander (cilantro) leaves, to garnish

1 Soak the dried Chinese mushrooms, if using, for at least 30 minutes in 300 ml/ ½ pint/1¼ cups of the vegetable stock. Remove the stalks and discard, then slice the mushrooms. Reserve the stock.

2 Cook the noodles for 2–3 minutes in boiling water. Drain and rinse. Set them aside.

3 ▼ Heat the oil over a high heat in a wok or large, heavy frying pan (skillet). Add the garlic and ginger, stir and add the mushrooms. Stir over a high heat for 2 minutes.

4 ▼ Add the remaining vegetable stock to the wok or pan, along with the reserved vegetable stock from the mushrooms, and bring to the boil. Add the mushroom ketchup and soy sauce.

5 ▼ Stir in the bean-sprouts and cook until tender.

6 Spoon the soup over the noodles, garnish with coriander (cilantro) leaves and serve immediately.

LETTUCE & TOFU (BEAN CURD) SOUP

This is a delicate, clear soup of shredded lettuce and small chunks of tofu (bean curd) with sliced carrot and spring onion (scallion).

SERVES 4

INGREDIENTS:
200 g/7 oz tofu (bean curd)
2 tbsp vegetable oil
1 carrot, sliced thinly
1 cm/½ inch piece ginger root, cut into thin shreds
3 spring onions (scallions), sliced diagonally
1.25 litres/2 pints/5 cups vegetable stock
2 tbsp soy sauce
2 tbsp dry sherry
1 tsp sugar
125 g/4 oz/1½ cups cos (romaine) lettuce, shredded
salt and pepper

1 ▼ Cut the tofu (bean curd) into small cubes. Heat the oil in a wok or large saucepan, add the tofu (bean curd) and stir-fry until browned. Remove with a slotted spoon and drain on paper towels.

2 ▲ Add the carrot, ginger root and spring onions (scallions) to the wok or saucepan and stir-fry for 2 minutes.

3 Add the stock, soy sauce, sherry and sugar. Bring to the boil and simmer for 1 minute.

4 ▼ Add the lettuce and stir until it has just wilted.

5 Return the tofu (bean curd) to the wok or saucepan to reheat. Season with salt and pepper and serve in warmed bowls.

THAI-STYLE CHICKEN & COCONUT SOUP

This fragrant soup has the complex flavours so typical of Thai food. It combines the citrus flavours of lemon grass and lime with coconut and a hint of piquancy comes from the fresh red chillies.

SERVES 4

INGREDIENTS:
350 g/12 oz/1¾ cups cooked, skinned
  chicken breast
125 g/4 oz/1⅓ cups unsweetened
  desiccated (shredded) coconut
500 ml/16 fl oz/2 cups boiling water
500 ml/16 fl oz/2 cups chicken stock
4 spring onions (scallions), white and
  green parts, sliced thinly
2 stalks lemon grass
1 lime
1 tsp grated ginger root
1 tbsp light soy sauce
2 tsp ground coriander
2 large red chillies
1 tbsp chopped fresh coriander
  (cilantro)
1 tbsp cornflour (cornstarch) mixed
  with 2 tbsp cold water
salt and white pepper
chopped red chilli, to garnish

1 ▼ Slice the chicken into thin strips. Place the coconut in a heatproof bowl and pour the boiling water over.

2 ▲ Place a fine sieve (strainer) over another bowl and pour in the coconut water. Work the coconut through the sieve (strainer). Pour the coconut water into a large saucepan and add the stock.

3 ▲ Add the spring onions (scallions) to the saucepan. Slice the base of each lemon grass and discard any damaged leaves. Bruise the stalks and add to the saucepan.

4 Peel the rind from the whole lime, keeping it in large strips. Slice the lime in half and extract the juice. Add the lime strips, lime juice, grated ginger, soy sauce and ground coriander to the saucepan.

5 ▲ Bruise the chillies with a fork, then add to the saucepan. Heat the contents of the pan to just below the boiling point.

6 Add the chicken strips and fresh coriander (cilantro) to the saucepan, bring to the boil, then simmer for 10 minutes.

7 Discard the lemon grass, lime rind and chillies. Pour the blended cornflour (cornstarch) mixture into the saucepan and stir until slightly thickened. Season to taste, then serve, garnished with chopped red chilli.

HOT & SOUR SOUP

A very traditional staple of the Thai national diet, and quite different from the Chinese soup of the same name, this soup is sold on street corners, at food bars and by mobile vendors all over Thailand.

SERVES 4

INGREDIENTS:
1 tbsp sunflower oil
250 g/8 oz smoked tofu (bean curd), sliced
90 g/3 oz/1 cup shiitake mushrooms, sliced
2 tbsp chopped fresh coriander (cilantro)
125 g/4 oz/2 cups watercress
1 red chilli, sliced finely, to garnish

STOCK:
1 tbsp tamarind pulp
2 dried red chillies, chopped
2 kaffir lime leaves, torn in half
2.5 cm/1 inch piece ginger root, chopped
5 cm/2 inch piece galangal, chopped
1 stalk lemon grass, chopped
1 onion, quartered
1 litre/1¾ pints/4 cups cold water

1 ▼ Put all the ingredients for the stock into a saucepan and bring to the boil. Simmer for 5 minutes. Remove the pan from the heat and strain, reserving the stock.

2 ▼ Heat the oil in a wok or large, heavy frying pan (skillet) and cook the tofu (bean curd) over a high heat for about 2 minutes, stirring constantly. Add the strained stock.

3 ▼ Add the mushrooms and coriander (cilantro), and boil for 3 minutes. Add the watercress and boil for 1 minute. Serve immediately, garnished with red chilli slices.

SWEETCORN & CRAB MEAT SOUP

You must use American-style creamed sweetcorn for this soup since the recipe originated in the USA! Chicken can be used instead of the crab meat, if preferred.

SERVES 4

INGREDIENTS:
125 g/4 oz crab meat
¼ tsp finely chopped ginger root
2 egg whites
2 tbsp milk
1 tbsp cornflour (cornstarch) paste
*   (see page 15)*
600 ml/1 pint/2 ½ cups Chinese Stock
*   (see page 10)*
250 g/8 oz can American-style creamed
*   sweetcorn*
salt and pepper
finely chopped spring onions (scallions),
*   to garnish*

1 Flake the crab meat (or coarsely chop the chicken breast) and mix with the ginger.

2 ▼ Beat the egg whites until frothy, add the milk and cornflour (cornstarch) paste and beat again until smooth. Blend in the crab or chicken.

3 ▲ In a wok or large frying pan (skillet), bring the stock to the boil, add the creamed sweetcorn and bring back to the boil.

4 ▼ Stir in the crab meat or chicken pieces and egg-white mixture, adjust the seasoning and stir gently until the mixture is well blended. Serve hot, garnished with chopped spring onions (scallions).

WONTON SOUP

Spinach and pine kernel (nut) filled wontons are served in a clear soup. The recipe for the wonton skins makes 24 but the soup requires only half this quantity. The other half can be frozen, ready for another time.

SERVES 4

INGREDIENTS:
WONTON SKINS:
1 egg
6 tbsp water
250 g/8 oz/2 cups plain (all-purpose)
*   flour*

FILLING:
125 g/4 oz/½ cup frozen chopped
*   spinach, defrosted*
15 g/½ oz/1 tbsp pine kernels (nuts),
*   toasted and chopped*
30 g/1 oz/¼ cup minced quorn (TVP)
salt

SOUP:
600 ml/1 pint/2½ cups vegetable stock
1 tbsp dry sherry
1 tbsp light soy sauce
2 spring onions (scallions), chopped

1 ▼ Beat the egg lightly in a bowl and mix with the water. Stir in the flour to form a stiff dough. Knead lightly, then cover with a damp cloth and leave to rest for 30 minutes.

2 Roll the dough out into a large sheet about 1.5 mm/¼ inch thick. Cut out 24 squares, 7 cm/3 inch. Dust each one lightly with flour. Only 12 squares are required for the soup, so freeze the remainder.

3 ▲ To make the filling, squeeze out the excess water from the frozen spinach. Mix the spinach with the pine kernels (nuts) and quorn (TVP). Season with salt.

4 ▲ Divide the mixture into 12 equal portions and place one portion in the centre of each square. Seal by bringing the opposite corners of each square together and squeezing well.

5 To make the soup, bring the stock, sherry and soy sauce to the boil, add the wontons and boil rapidly for 2–3 minutes. Add the spring onions (scallions) and serve immediately in warmed bowls.

THREE-FLAVOUR SOUP

Ideally, use raw prawns (shrimp) in this soup. If that is not possible, add ready-cooked ones at the very last stage.

SERVES 4

INGREDIENTS:
125 g/4 oz skinned, boned chicken breast
125 g/4 oz raw peeled prawns (shrimp)
125 g/4 oz honey-roast ham
½ egg white, lightly beaten
2 tsp cornflour (cornstarch) paste (see page 15)
750 ml/1¼ pints/3 cups Chinese Stock (see page 10) or water
salt and pepper
finely chopped spring onions (scallions), to garnish

1 ▲ Thinly slice the chicken into small shreds. If the prawns (shrimp) are large, cut each in half lengthways, otherwise leave whole.

2 ▲ Cut the ham into small thin slices roughly the same size as the chicken.

3 ▼ Place the chicken and prawns (shrimps) in a bowl and mix with a pinch of salt, the egg white and cornflour (cornstarch) paste until well coated.

4 Bring the stock or water to a rolling boil.

5 ▼ Add the chicken, the raw prawns (shrimps) and the ham. Bring the soup back to the boil, and simmer for 1 minute.

6 Adjust the seasoning and serve the soup hot, garnished with the spring onions (scallions).

NOODLE & RICE DISHES

Rice may well be the staple food in the East, but freshly cooked plain long-grain rice is only one way of serving it. In countless other dishes it is baked, steamed, stir-fried and boiled with an almost infinite spectrum of vegetables, herbs, spices and flavourings to entice and delight. Noodles, too, have a major role to play, and many, simply fried with just a few extra ingredients, make superb light meals to enjoy in their own right. Noodles are served throughout the day, even for breakfast, and can be boiled, deep-fried, stir-fried with vegetables or meat, served with a sauce or cooked in a soup. Some of the following recipes make ideal side dishes to accompany a more substantial main dish of meat or fish, whereas others would make a meal in themselves, such as the Singapore-style Rice Noodles or the Seafood Chow Mein. In China fried rice and chow mein are only served at formal occasions or as a snack between main meals, but there is no need for the Western cook to follow oriental customs so exactly – try serving both a rice and noodle dish at a meal.

CHATUCHAK FRIED RICE (PAGE 46)

SINGAPORE-STYLE RICE NOODLES

Rice noodles or vermicelli are also known as rice sticks. Egg noodles can be used for this dish, but it will not taste the same.

SERVES 4

INGREDIENTS:
200 g/7 oz rice vermicelli
125 g/4 oz cooked chicken or pork
60 g/2 oz peeled prawns (shrimp),
   defrosted if frozen
4 tbsp vegetable oil
1 medium onion, thinly shredded
125 g/4 oz fresh bean-sprouts
1 tsp salt
1 tbsp mild curry powder
2 tbsp light soy sauce
2 spring onions (scallions), shredded
1–2 small fresh green or red chilli
   peppers, deseeded and shredded

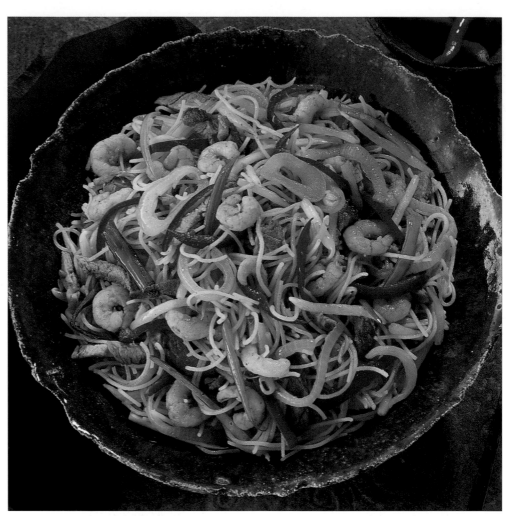

1 ▲ Soak the rice vermicelli in boiling water for 8–10 minutes, then rinse in cold water and drain well.

2 ▼ Thinly slice the cooked meat. Dry the prawns (shrimp) on paper towels.

3 ▲ Heat the oil in a preheated wok. Add the onion and stir-fry until opaque. Add the bean-sprouts and stir-fry for 1 minute.

4 ▲ Add the noodles with the meat and prawns (shrimp), and continue stirring for another minute.

5 Blend in the salt, curry powder and soy sauce, followed by the spring onions (scallions) and chilli peppers. Stir-fry for one more minute, then serve immediately.

CRISPY DEEP-FRIED NOODLES

This is the staple dish on every Thai restaurant menu by which the establishment will be judged. It does require a certain amount of care and attention to get the crispy noodles properly cooked.

SERVES 4

INGREDIENTS:
175 g/6 oz thread egg noodles
600 ml/1 pint/2½ cups sunflower oil for deep-frying
2 tsp grated lemon rind
1 tbsp light soy sauce
1 tbsp rice vinegar
1 tbsp lemon juice
1¼ tbsp sugar
250 g/8 oz/1 cup marinated tofu (bean curd), diced
2 garlic cloves, crushed
1 red chilli, sliced finely
1 red (bell) pepper, diced
4 eggs, beaten
sliced red chilli, to garnish

1 ▼ Blanch the egg noodles briefly in hot water, to which a little of the oil has been added. Drain and spread out to dry for at least 30 minutes. Cut into threads about 7 cm/3 inches long.

2 Combine the lemon rind, light soy sauce, rice vinegar, lemon juice and sugar in a small bowl.

3 ▲ Heat the oil in a wok or large, heavy frying pan (skillet), and test the temperature with a few strands of noodles. They should swell to many times their size, but if they do not, wait until the oil is hot enough; otherwise they will be tough and stringy, not puffy and light. Cook them in batches. As soon as they turn a pale gold colour, scoop them out and drain on plenty of paper towels. Leave to cool.

4 ▼ Reserve 2 tablespoons of the oil and drain off the rest. Heat the 2 tablespoons of oil in the wok or pan (skillet). Cook the tofu (bean curd) quickly over a high heat to seal. Add the garlic, chilli and diced (bell) pepper. Stir for 1–2 minutes. Add the vinegar mixture to the pan, stir, then add the eggs, stirring until they are set.

5 Serve with the crispy fried noodles, garnished with sliced red chilli.

ORIENTAL VEGETABLE NOODLES

This dish has a mild, nutty flavour from the peanut butter and dry-roasted peanuts.

SERVES 4

INGREDIENTS:
175 g/6 oz/1¼ cups green thread noodles or multi-coloured spaghetti
125 g/4 oz daikon (mooli), grated
125 g/4 oz/1 large carrot, grated
125 g/4 oz cucumber, shredded finely
1 bunch spring onions (scallions), shredded finely
1 tbsp dry-roasted peanuts, crushed

PEANUT DRESSING:
1 tsp sesame oil
2 tbsp crunchy peanut butter
2 tbsp light soy sauce
1 tbsp white wine vinegar
1 tsp clear honey
salt and pepper

TO GARNISH:
carrot flowers
spring onion (scallion) tassels

1 ▼ Bring a large saucepan of water to the boil, add the noodles or spaghetti and cook according to the packet instructions. Drain well and rinse in cold water. Leave in a bowl of cold water until required.

2 Make the dressing. Put the sesame oil, peanut butter, soy sauce, vinegar, honey and seasoning into a small screw-top jar. Seal and shake well.

3 ▼ Drain the noodles or spaghetti well, place in a large serving bowl and mix in half the peanut dressing.

4 ▼ Using 2 forks, toss the daikon (mooli), carrot, cucumber and spring onions (scallions) into the bowl.

5 Sprinkle with crushed peanuts and garnish with carrot flowers and spring onion (scallion) tassels. Serve with the remaining peanut dressing.

HOMEMADE NOODLES WITH STIR-FRIED VEGETABLES

These noodles are simple to make; you do not need a pasta-making machine or any specialist equipment as the noodles are rolled out by hand.

SERVES 2–4

INGREDIENTS:
NOODLES:
125 g/4 oz/1 cup plain (all-purpose) flour
2 tbsp cornflour (cornstarch)
½ tsp salt
120 ml/4 fl oz/½ cup boiling water
5 tbsp vegetable oil

STIR-FRY:
1 courgette (zucchini)
1 celery stick
1 carrot
125 g/4 oz open-cup mushrooms
1 leek
125 g/4 oz broccoli
125 g/4 oz/2 cups bean-sprouts
1 tbsp soy sauce
2 tsp rice vinegar (if unavailable, use white wine vinegar)
½ tsp sugar

1 ▼ To prepare the noodles, sift the flour, cornflour (cornstarch) and salt into a bowl. Make a well in the centre and pour in the boiling water and 1 teaspoon of the oil. Mix quickly, using a wooden spoon, to make a soft dough. Cover and leave for 5–6 minutes.

2 Prepare the vegetables for the stir-fry. Cut the courgette (zucchini), celery and carrot into thin sticks. Slice the mushrooms and leek. Divide the broccoli into small florets and peel and thinly slice the stalks.

3 ▲ Make the noodles by breaking off small pieces of dough and rolling into balls. Then roll each ball across a very lightly oiled work surface (counter) with the palm of your hand to form thin noodles. Do not worry if some of the noodles break into shorter lengths. Set the noodles aside.

4 Heat 3 tablespoons of oil in a wok or large frying pan (skillet). Add the noodles in batches and fry over a high heat for 1 minute. Reduce the heat and cook for a further 2 minutes. Remove and drain on paper towels. Set aside.

5 ▼ Heat the remaining oil in the pan. Add the courgette (zucchini), celery and carrot, and stir-fry for 1 minute. Add the mushrooms, broccoli and leek, and stir-fry for a further minute. Stir in the remaining ingredients and mix well until thoroughly heated.

6 Add the noodles and toss to mix over a high heat. Serve immediately.

SESAME HOT NOODLES

Plain egg noodles are all the better when tossed in a dressing made with nutty sesame oil, soy sauce, peanut butter, coriander (cilantro), lime juice, chilli and sesame seeds. Serve hot as an accompaniment to a main meal.

SERVES 6

INGREDIENTS:
2 x 250 g/8 oz packets medium egg
   noodles
3 tbsp sunflower oil
2 tbsp sesame oil
1 garlic clove, crushed
1 tbsp smooth peanut butter
1 small green chilli, deseeded and very
   finely chopped
3 tbsp toasted sesame seeds
4 tbsp light soy sauce
1–2 tbsp lime juice
salt and pepper
4 tbsp chopped fresh coriander
   (cilantro)

1 ▼ Place the noodles in a large pan of boiling water, then immediately remove from the heat. Cover and leave to stand for 6 minutes, stirring once halfway through. At the end of 6 minutes the noodles will be perfectly cooked. Otherwise follow the packet instructions.

2 Meanwhile, mix the sunflower and sesame oils with the garlic and peanut butter until smooth.

3 ▼ Add the chilli, sesame seeds, soy sauce and lime juice, according to taste, and mix well. Season with salt and pepper.

4 ▼ Drain the noodles thoroughly, then place in a heated serving bowl. Add the dressing and coriander (cilantro) and toss well to mix. Serve immediately.

FRIED NOODLES WITH
BEAN-SPROUTS, CHIVES & CHILLI

This is a simple idea to jazz up noodles to accompany Thai or other oriental main course dishes.

SERVES 4

INGREDIENTS:
500 g/1 lb medium egg noodles
60 g/2 oz/1 cup bean-sprouts
15 g/½ oz chives
3 tbsp sunflower oil
1 garlic clove, crushed
4 green chillies, deseeded, sliced and
  soaked in 2 tbsp rice vinegar
salt

1 ▼ To cook the noodles, soak in boiling water for 10 minutes. Drain and set aside.

2 ▼ Soak the bean-sprouts in cold water while you cut the chives into 2.5cm/1 inch pieces. Set a few chives aside for garnish. Drain the bean-sprouts thoroughly.

3 Heat the oil in a wok or large, heavy frying pan (skillet). Add the crushed garlic and stir briefly.

4 ▼ Add the chillies to the wok or pan (skillet) and stir until fragrant, about 1 minute.

5 ▲ Add the bean-sprouts, stir and then add the noodles. Stir in some salt and the chives. Using 2 spoons, lift and stir the noodles for 1 minute.

6 Garnish the finished dish with the reserved chives, and serve at once.

SEAFOOD CHOW MEIN

Use whatever seafood is available for this delicious noodle dish – mussels or crab would also be suitable. Simply add to the wok with the other seafood in step 6.

SERVES 4

INGREDIENTS:
90 g/3 oz squid
3-4 fresh scallops
90 g/3 oz raw prawns (shrimp),
    shelled
½ egg white, lightly beaten
1 tbsp cornflour (cornstarch) paste
    (see page 15)
275 g/9 oz egg noodles
5-6 tbsp vegetable oil
2 tbsp light soy sauce
60 g/2 oz mangetout (snow peas)
½ tsp salt
½ tsp sugar
1 tsp Chinese rice wine or dry sherry
2 spring onions (scallions), finely
    shredded
few drops of sesame oil

1 First clean the squid. Cut off the head. Cut off the tentacles and reserve. Remove the small bone at the base of the tentacles and the transparent backbone, as well as the ink bag. Peel off the thin skin, then wash and dry.

2 ▼ Open up the squid and score the inside in a criss-cross pattern, then cut into pieces about the size of a postage stamp.

3 ▼ Soak the squid in a bowl of boiling water until all the pieces curl up. Rinse in cold water and drain.

4 Cut each scallop into 3–4 slices. Cut the prawns (shrimp) in half lengthways if they are large. Mix the scallops and prawns with the egg white and cornflour (cornstarch) paste in a bowl.

5 Cook the noodles in boiling water according to the instructions on the packet, then drain and rinse under cold water. Drain well, then toss with about 1 tablespoon of oil.

6 ▼ Heat 3 tablespoons of oil in a preheated wok. Add the noodles and 1 tablespoon of the soy sauce and stir-fry for 2-3 minutes. Remove to a large serving dish.

7 Heat the remaining oil in the wok and add the mangetout (snow peas) and seafood. Stir-fry for about 2 minutes, then add the salt, sugar, wine, remaining soy sauce and about half the spring onions (scallions). Blend well and add a little stock or water if necessary.

8 Pour the seafood mixture on top of the noodles and sprinkle with sesame oil. Garnish with the remaining spring onions (scallions) and serve hot or cold.

EGG FU-YUNG WITH RICE

In this dish, cooked rice is mixed with scrambled eggs, Chinese mushrooms, bamboo shoots and water chestnuts, and it is a great way of using up leftover cooked rice. It can be served as a meal by itself or as an accompaniment.

SERVES 2–4

INGREDIENTS:

175 g/6 oz/generous ¾ cup long-grain rice
2 Chinese dried mushrooms (if unavailable, use thinly sliced open-cup mushrooms)
3 eggs, beaten
3 tbsp vegetable oil
4 spring onions (scallions), sliced
¼ green (bell) pepper, chopped
60 g/2 oz/⅓ cup canned bamboo shoots
60 g/2 oz/⅓ cup canned water chestnuts, sliced
125 g/4 oz/2 cups bean-sprouts
2 tbsp light soy sauce
2 tbsp dry sherry
2 tsp sesame oil
salt and pepper

1 Cook the rice in lightly salted boiling water according to the packet instructions.

2 ▲ Place the dried mushrooms in a small bowl, cover with warm water and leave to soak for 20–25 minutes.

3 ▼ Mix the beaten eggs with a little salt. Heat 1 tablespoon of the oil in a wok or large frying pan (skillet). Add the eggs and stir until just set. Remove and set aside.

4 Drain the mushrooms and squeeze out the excess water. Remove the tough centres and chop the mushrooms.

5 Heat the remaining oil in a clean wok or frying pan (skillet). Add the mushrooms, spring onions (scallions) and green (bell) pepper, and stir-fry for 2 minutes. Add the bamboo shoots, water chestnuts and bean-sprouts. Stir-fry for 1 minute.

6 ▲ Drain the rice thoroughly and add to the pan with the remaining ingredients. Mix well, heating the rice thoroughly. Season to taste with salt and pepper. Stir in the reserved eggs and serve.

FRAGRANT STEAMED RICE IN LOTUS LEAVES

The fragrance of the leaves penetrates the rice, giving it a unique taste. Lotus leaves can be bought from specialist oriental shops. Large cabbage or spinach leaves can be used as a substitute.

SERVES 4

INGREDIENTS:

2 lotus leaves
4 Chinese dried mushrooms (if unavailable, use thinly sliced open-cup mushrooms)
175 g/6 oz/generous ¾ cup long-grain rice
1 cinnamon stick
6 cardamom pods
4 cloves
1 tsp salt
2 eggs
1 tbsp vegetable oil
2 spring onions (scallions), chopped
1 tbsp soy sauce
2 tbsp sherry
1 tsp sugar
1 tsp sesame oil

1 ▼ Unfold the lotus leaves carefully and cut along the fold to divide each leaf in half. Lay on a large baking sheet and pour over enough hot water to cover. Leave to soak for about 30 minutes or until the lotus leaves have softened.

2 Place the dried mushrooms in a small bowl and cover with warm water. Leave the mushrooms to soak for 20–25 minutes.

3 Cook the long-grain rice in plenty of boiling water in a saucepan with the cinnamon stick, cardamom pods, cloves and salt for about 10 minutes – the rice should be partially cooked. Drain thoroughly and remove the cinnamon stick.

4 ▲ Beat the eggs lightly. Heat the oil in a wok or frying pan (skillet) and cook the eggs quickly, stirring constantly until set; then remove and set aside.

5 Drain the mushrooms, squeezing out the excess water. Remove the tough centres and chop the mushrooms.

6 Place the drained rice in a large bowl. Stir in the chopped mushrooms, cooked egg, spring onions (scallions), soy sauce, sherry, sugar and sesame oil. Season with salt to taste.

7 ▼ Drain the lotus leaves and divide the rice mixture into four portions. Place a portion in the centre of each lotus leaf and fold up to form a parcel (package).

8 Place the lotus leaf parcels in a steamer, cover and steam over simmering water for 20 minutes. To serve, cut the tops of the lotus leaves open to expose the fragrant rice inside.

THAI FRAGRANT COCONUT RICE

This is the finest rice to serve with Thai-style food. Basmati rice is cooked with creamed coconut, lemon grass, fresh ginger and spices to make a wonderfully aromatic, fluffy rice. When using lemon grass, beat it well to bruise it before slicing or chopping so the flavour is fully released.

SERVES 4–6

INGREDIENTS:

2.5 cm/1 inch piece ginger root, peeled
  and sliced
2 cloves
1 stalk lemon grass, bruised and halved
2 tsp ground nutmeg
1 cinnamon stick
1 bay leaf
2 small thin strips lime rind
1 tsp salt
30 g/1 oz creamed coconut, chopped
600 ml/1 pint/2½ cups water
350 g/12 oz/1¾ cups basmati rice
pepper

1 ▼ Place the ginger, cloves, lemon grass, nutmeg, cinnamon stick, bay leaf, lime rind, salt, creamed coconut and water in a large, heavy-based pan and bring slowly to the boil.

2 ▼ Add the rice, stir well, then cover and simmer, over a very gentle heat, for about 15 minutes or until all the liquid has been absorbed and the rice is tender but still has a bite to it.

3 ▲ Remove from the heat, add pepper to taste, then fluff up the rice with a fork. Remove the large pieces of spices before serving.

NASI GORENG

An Indonesian rice dish flavoured with vegetables and pork, soy sauce and curry spices with strips of omelette added as a topping.

SERVES 4

INGREDIENTS:
300 g/10 oz/1½ cups long-grain rice
350–500 g/12 oz–1 lb pork fillet or lean
    pork slices
3 tomatoes, skinned, quartered and
    deseeded
2 eggs
4 tsp water
3 tbsp sunflower oil
1 onion, thinly sliced
1–2 garlic cloves, crushed
1 tsp medium or mild curry powder
¼ tsp ground coriander
¼ tsp medium chilli powder or 1 tsp
    bottled sweet chilli sauce
2 tbsp soy sauce
125 g/4 oz frozen peas, defrosted
salt and pepper

1 Cook the rice in boiling salted water, following the packet instructions and keep warm.

2 Meanwhile, cut the pork into narrow strips across the grain, discarding any fat. Slice the tomatoes.

3 ▲ Beat each egg separately with 2 teaspoons cold water and salt and pepper. Heat 2 teaspoons of oil in the wok, swirling it around until really hot. Pour in the first egg, swirl it around and cook undisturbed until set.

4 Remove to a plate or board and repeat with the second egg. Cut the omelettes into strips about 1 cm/½ in wide.

5 ▼ Heat the remaining oil in the wok and when really hot add the onion and garlic and stir-fry for 1–2 minutes. Add the pork and continue to stir-fry for about 3 minutes or until almost cooked.

6 Add the curry powder, coriander, chilli powder or chilli sauce and soy sauce to the wok and cook for a further minute, stirring constantly.

7 ▲ Stir in the rice, tomatoes and peas and stir-fry for about 2 minutes until piping hot. Adjust the seasoning and turn into a heated serving dish. Arrange the strips of omelette on top and serve at once.

GREEN RICE

A deliciously different way to serve plain rice for a special occasion or to liven up a simple meal.

SERVES 4

INGREDIENTS:
2 tbsp olive oil
500 g/1 lb/2¼ cups basmati or Thai jasmine rice, soaked for 1 hour, washed and drained
750 ml/1¼ pints/3 cups coconut milk
1 tsp salt
1 bay leaf
2 tbsp chopped fresh coriander (cilantro)
2 tbsp chopped fresh mint
2 green chillies, deseeded and chopped finely

1 ▼ Heat the oil in a saucepan, add the rice and stir until it becomes translucent.

2 ▲ Add the coconut milk, salt and bay leaf. Bring to the boil and cook until all the liquid is absorbed.

3 ▼ Lower the heat as much as possible, cover the saucepan tightly and cook for 10 minutes. Remove the bay leaf.

4 ▲ Stir in the chopped coriander (cilantro), mint and green chillies. Fork through the rice gently and serve immediately.

SPECIAL FRIED RICE

In this simple recipe, cooked rice is fried with vegetables and cashew nuts. It can either be eaten on its own or served as an accompaniment.

SERVES 2–4

INGREDIENTS:
175 g/6 oz/generous ¾ cup long-grain rice
60 g/2 oz/½ cup cashew nuts
1 carrot
½ cucumber
1 yellow (bell) pepper
2 spring onions (scallions)
2 tbsp vegetable oil
1 garlic clove, crushed
125 g/4 oz/¾ cup frozen peas, defrosted
1 tbsp soy sauce
1 tsp salt
coriander (cilantro) leaves, to garnish

1 Bring a large pan of water to the boil. Add the rice and simmer for 15 minutes. Tip the rice into a sieve (strainer) and rinse; drain thoroughly.

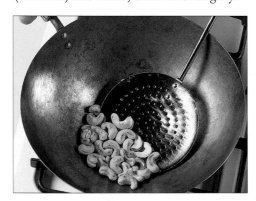

2 ▲ Heat a wok or large frying pan (skillet), add the cashew nuts and dry-fry until lightly browned. Remove and set aside.

3 ▲ Cut the carrot in half along the length, then slice thinly into semi-circles. Halve the cucumber and remove the seeds, using a teaspoon, then dice the cucumber. Slice the yellow (bell) pepper and chop the spring onions (scallions).

4 ▼ Heat the oil in the wok or large frying pan (skillet). Add the prepared vegetables and the garlic. Stir-fry for 3 minutes. Add the rice, peas, soy sauce and salt. Continue to stir-fry until well mixed and heated through.

5 Stir in the reserved cashew nuts and serve garnished with coriander (cilantro) leaves.

CHINESE FRIED RICE

The rice for this dish may be cooked in the wok or conventionally in a saucepan, but it is essential to use cold, dry rice with separate grains to make this recipe properly.

SERVES 4–6

INGREDIENTS:
750 ml/1¼ pints/3 cups water
½ tsp salt
300 g/10 oz/1½ cups long-grain rice
2 eggs
4 tsp cold water
3 tbsp sunflower oil
4 spring onions (scallions), sliced diagonally
1 red, green or yellow (bell) pepper, cored, deseeded and thinly sliced
3-4 lean slices bacon, rind removed, cut into strips
200 g/7 oz fresh bean-sprouts
125 g/4 oz frozen peas, defrosted
2 tbsp soy sauce (optional)
salt and pepper

1 Pour the water into the wok with the salt and bring to the boil. Rinse the rice in a sieve under cold water until the water runs clear, drain well and add to the boiling water. Stir well, then cover the wok tightly with the lid or a lid made of foil, and simmer gently for 12–13 minutes. (Don't remove the lid during cooking.)

2 ▼ Remove the lid, give the rice a good stir and then spread it out on a large plate, tray or baking sheet to cool and dry.

3 Beat one egg in a small bowl with salt and pepper and 2 teaspoons cold water. Heat 1 tablespoon of the oil in the wok, swirling it around until really hot. Pour in the egg, swirl it around and leave to cook undisturbed until set. Remove the cooked omelette to a board or plate, and repeat the whole process with the second egg.

4 ▲ Roll up each omelette and cut it across into thin slices.

5 ▼ Add the remaining oil to the wok and when really hot add the spring onions (scallions) and (bell) pepper and stir-fry for 1–2 minutes. Add the bacon and continue to stir-fry for a further 1–2 minutes. Add the bean-sprouts and peas and toss together thoroughly; stir in the soy sauce if using.

6 Add the rice and seasoning and stir-fry for a minute or so then add the strips of omelette and continue to stir for about 2 minutes or until the rice is piping hot. Serve at once.

CHATUCHAK FRIED RICE

An excellent way to use up leftover rice! Freeze it as soon as it is cool. It will be ready to use at any time. This dish should be reheated only once.

SERVES 4

✽✽✽✽✽✽✽✽✽✽✽

INGREDIENTS:
1 tbsp sunflower oil
3 shallots, chopped finely
2 garlic cloves, crushed
1 red chilli, deseeded and chopped finely
2.5 cm/1 inch piece ginger root, shredded finely
½ green (bell) pepper, sliced finely
150 g/5 oz/2–3 baby aubergines (eggplants), quartered
90 g/3 oz sugar snap peas or mangetout (snow peas), trimmed and blanched
90 g/3 oz/6 baby sweetcorn, halved lengthways and blanched
1 tomato, cut into 8 pieces
90 g/3 oz/1½ cups bean-sprouts
500 g/1 lb/3 cups cooked Thai jasmine rice
2 tbsp tomato ketchup
2 tbsp light soy sauce

TO GARNISH:
coriander (cilantro) leaves
lime wedges

✽✽✽✽✽✽✽✽✽✽✽✽

1 ▲ Heat the sunflower oil in a wok or large, heavy frying pan (skillet) over a high heat. Add the shallots, garlic, chilli and ginger. Stir until the shallots have softened.

2 Add the green (bell) pepper and baby aubergines (eggplants) and stir.

3 ▼ Add the sugar snap peas or mangetout (snow peas), baby sweetcorn, tomato pieces and bean-sprouts. Stir for 3 minutes.

4 ▲ Add the rice, and lift and stir with 2 spoons for 4–5 minutes, until no more steam is released. Stir in the tomato ketchup and soy sauce.

5 Serve immediately, garnished with coriander (cilantro) and lime wedges.

VEGETABLE & VEGETARIAN DISHES

The Eastern diet is rich in vegetables, and many meat and poultry dishes include some kind of vegetable as a supplementary ingredient. An astonishing range of vegetables is found in the East, many which are not available to Westerners, such as the numerous varieties of aubergine (eggplant) found in Thailand in every size, shape and colour. When selecting vegetables for cooking, choose very fresh ingredients, wash them just before cutting or chopping, then cook them as soon as they have been cut so the vitamin content is not lost. Some of the recipes in this chapter, such as the Green Curry with Tempeh or the Vegetable & Nut Stir-Fry, are ideal to serve as a vegetarian main course. Others, such as Spinach with Straw Mushrooms, are best served as side dishes to complement the richer textures and more complex flavours of a main-course dish. Salads are also featured in this chapter and, while most of these are best served as an accompaniment, some make delicious light lunches on their own.

VEGETABLE & NUT STIR-FRY

A colourful selection of vegetables are stir-fried in a creamy peanut sauce and sprinkled with nuts to serve.

SERVES 4

❀❀❀❀❀❀❀❀❀❀❀❀❀❀❀❀❀❀❀❀

INGREDIENTS:
3 tbsp crunchy peanut butter
150 ml/¼ pint/⅔ cup water
1 tbsp soy sauce
1 tsp sugar
1 carrot
¼ red onion
4 baby courgettes (zucchini)
1 red (bell) pepper
250 g/8 oz egg thread noodles
30 g/1 oz/¼ cup peanuts, chopped
   roughly
2 tbsp vegetable oil
1 tsp sesame oil
1 small green chilli, deseeded and sliced
   thinly
1 garlic clove, sliced thinly
225 g/7½ oz can of water chestnuts,
   drained and sliced
175 g/6 oz/3 cups bean-sprouts
salt

❀❀❀❀❀❀❀❀❀❀❀❀❀❀❀❀❀❀❀❀

1 ▼ Gradually blend the peanut butter with the water in a small bowl. Stir in the soy sauce and sugar.

2 Cut the carrot into thin matchsticks and slice the onion. Slice the courgettes (zucchini) on the diagonal and cut the (bell) pepper into chunks.

3 Bring a large pan of water to the boil and add the egg noodles. Remove from the heat immediately and leave to rest for 4 minutes, stirring occasionally to divide the noodles.

4 ▼ Heat a wok or large frying pan (skillet), add the peanuts and dry-fry until they are beginning to brown. Remove and set aside.

5 ▼ Add the vegetable and sesame oils to the pan and heat. Add the carrot, onion, courgette (zucchini), (bell) pepper, chilli and garlic, and stir-fry for 2–3 minutes. Add the water chestnuts, bean-sprouts and peanut sauce. Bring to the boil and heat thoroughly. Season to taste. Drain the noodles and serve with the stir-fry. Sprinkle with the peanuts.

SWEETCORN PATTIES

These little patties are very simple to prepare. They can be served as a light lunch or a starter, but also make a delicious addition to a party buffet. Serve them with a sweet chilli sauce.

MAKES 12

INGREDIENTS:

*325 g/11 oz can sweetcorn, drained
1 onion, chopped finely
1 tsp curry powder
1 garlic clove, crushed
1 tsp ground coriander
2 spring onions (scallions), chopped
3 tbsp plain (all-purpose) flour
¼ tsp baking powder
salt
1 large egg
4 tbsp sunflower oil*

1 ▲ Mash the drained sweetcorn lightly in a medium-sized bowl.

2 ▼ Then add all the remaining ingredients, except for the sunflower oil, one at a time and stirring after each addition.

3 ▼ Heat the sunflower oil in a large frying pan (skillet). Drop rounded tablespoonfuls of the sweetcorn mixture carefully on to the hot oil, spacing them far enough apart so the patties do not to run into each other as they cook.

4 ▲ Cook for 4–5 minutes, turning each patty once, until they are golden brown and firm. Take care not to turn them too soon, or they will break up.

5 Remove from the pan and drain on paper towels. Serve while still warm.

AUBERGINES (EGGPLANTS) IN CHILLI SAUCE

Strips of aubergine (eggplant) are deep-fried, then served in a fragrant chilli sauce.

SERVES 4

❁❁❁❁❁❁❁❁❁❁❁❁❁❁❁❁❁

INGREDIENTS:
1 large aubergine (eggplant)
vegetable oil, for deep-frying
2 carrots
4 spring onions (scallions)
2 large garlic cloves
1 tbsp vegetable oil
2 tsp chilli sauce
1 tbsp soy sauce
1 tbsp dry sherry

❁❁❁❁❁❁❁❁❁❁❁❁❁❁❁❁❁

1 ▼ Slice the aubergine (eggplant) and then cut into strips about the size of potato chips (French fries).

2 ▼ Heat enough oil in a heavy-based saucepan to deep-fry the aubergine (eggplant) in batches until just browned. The oil should be 180–190°C/350–375°F. Remove the strips with a perforated spoon and drain them on paper towels.

3 Cut the carrots into matchsticks. Trim and slice the spring onions (scallions) diagonally. Slice the garlic.

4 ▲ Heat 1 tablespoon of oil in a wok or large frying pan (skillet). Add the carrot and stir-fry for 1 minute; then add the spring onions (scallions) and garlic for a further minute.

5 ▲ Stir in the chilli sauce, soy sauce and sherry, then stir in the drained aubergine (eggplant). Mix well so that the vegetables are heated through thoroughly before serving.

GREEN CURRY WITH TEMPEH

There are three basic curries in Thai cuisine, of which the green curry is the hottest, red curry is medium and Massaman curry is the mildest. The green curry paste will keep for up to 3 weeks in the refrigerator. Serve over rice or noodles.

SERVES 4

INGREDIENTS:

1 tbsp sunflower oil
175 g/6 oz marinated or plain tempeh,
  cut into diamonds
6 spring onions (scallions), cut into
  2.5 cm/1 inch pieces
150 ml/¼ pint/⅔ cup coconut milk
Green Curry Paste
grated rind of 1 lime
15 g/½ oz/¼ cup fresh basil leaves
¼ tsp liquid seasoning, such as Maggi

GREEN CURRY PASTE:

2 tsp coriander seeds
1 tsp cumin seeds
1 tsp black peppercorns
4 large fresh green chillies, deseeded
2 shallots, quartered
2 garlic cloves, peeled
2 tbsp chopped fresh coriander
  (cilantro), including root and stalk
grated rind of 1 lime
1 tbsp roughly chopped galangal
1 tsp ground turmeric
salt
2 tbsp oil

TO GARNISH:

fresh coriander (cilantro) leaves
2 fresh green chillies, sliced thinly

1 To make the green curry paste, grind together the coriander and cumin seeds and the peppercorns in a food processor or pestle and mortar.

2 Blend the remaining ingredients together and add the ground spice mixture. Store in a clean, dry jar for up to 3 weeks in the refrigerator, or freeze in a suitable container. Makes 6 tbsp.

3 ▲ Heat the oil in a wok or large, heavy frying pan (skillet). Add the tempeh and stir over a high heat for about 2 minutes until sealed on all sides. Add the spring onions (scallions) and stir-fry for 1 minute. Remove the tempeh and spring onions (scallions) and reserve.

4 Put half the coconut milk into the wok or pan (skillet) and bring to the boil. Add the curry paste and lime rind, and cook until fragrant, about 1 minute. Add the reserved tempeh and spring onions (scallions).

5 ▼ Add the remaining coconut milk and simmer for 7–8 minutes. Stir in the basil leaves and liquid seasoning. Simmer for one more minute before serving, garnished with coriander (cilantro) and chillies.

CHINESE HOT SALAD

A mixture of vegetables stir-fried with a Chinese flavour, with an added touch of chilli. To serve cold, add 3–4 tablespoons French dressing as the vegetables cool, toss well and serve cold or chilled.

SERVES 4

INGREDIENTS:

1 tbsp dark soy sauce
1½–2 tsp bottled sweet chilli sauce
2 tbsp sherry
1 tbsp brown sugar
1 tbsp wine vinegar
2 tbsp sunflower oil
1 garlic clove, crushed
4 spring onions (scallions), thinly sliced diagonally
250 g/8 oz courgettes (zucchini) cut into julienne strips about 4 cm/ 1½ inches long
250 g/8 oz carrots, cut into julienne strips about 4 cm/1½ inches long
1 red or green (bell) pepper, cored, seeded and thinly sliced
400 g/14 oz can bean-sprouts, well drained
125 g/4 oz French or fine beans, cut into 5 cm/2 inch lengths
1 tbsp sesame oil
salt and pepper
1–2 tsp sesame seeds, to garnish

1 ▼ Blend the soy sauce, chilli sauce, sherry, sugar, vinegar and seasonings together.

2 Heat the 2 tablespoons of sunflower oil in a wok.

3 Add the garlic and spring onions (scallions) to the wok and stir-fry for 1–2 minutes.

4 ▲ Add the courgettes (zucchini), carrots and (bell) peppers and stir-fry for 1–2 minutes, then add the soy sauce mixture and bring to the boil.

5 ▲ Add the bean-sprouts and French beans and stir-fry for 1–2 minutes, making sure all the vegetables are thoroughly coated with the sauce.

6 Drizzle the sesame oil over the vegetables in the wok, stir-fry for about 30 seconds and serve hot sprinkled with sesame seeds.

GADO GADO SALAD

This salad is a mixture of cooked and raw vegetables served with a spicy peanut dressing.

SERVES 4

INGREDIENTS:
250 g/8 oz new potatoes, scrubbed
125 g/4 oz French (green) beans
125 g/4 oz cauliflower, broken into small florets
125 g/4 oz/1¼ cups white cabbage, shredded
1 carrot, cut into thin matchsticks
¼ cucumber, cut into chunks
125 g/4 oz/2 cups bean-sprouts
2 hard-boiled (hard-cooked) eggs

SAUCE:
6 tbsp crunchy peanut butter
300 ml/½ pint/1¼ cups cold water
1 garlic clove, crushed
1 red chilli, deseeded and finely chopped
2 tbsp soy sauce
1 tbsp dry sherry
2 tsp sugar
1 tbsp lemon juice

1 Halve the potatoes and place in a saucepan of lightly salted water. Bring to the boil and then simmer for 12–15 minutes, or until cooked through. Drain and plunge into cold water.

2 ▼ Bring another pan of lightly salted water to the boil. Add the French (green) beans, cauliflower and cabbage, and cook for 3 minutes. Drain and plunge into cold water.

3 ▼ Drain the vegetables. Arrange in piles on a large platter with the raw carrot, cucumber and bean-sprouts.

4 ▼ Shell the eggs, cut into quarters and arrange on the salad. Cover and set aside.

5 ▲ To make the sauce, place the peanut butter in a bowl and blend in the water gradually, followed by the remaining ingredients.

6 Uncover the salad, place the sauce in a separate serving bowl and drizzle some over each serving.

ORIENTAL SALAD

This colourful crisp salad has a fresh orange dressing and is topped with crunchy vermicelli.

SERVES 4–6

INGREDIENTS:
30 g/1 oz/¼ cup dried vermicelli
¼ head Chinese leaves
125 g/4 oz/2 cups bean-sprouts
6 radishes
125 g/4 oz mangetout (snow peas)
1 large carrot
125 g/4 oz sprouting beans

DRESSING:
5 tbsp fresh orange juice
1 tbsp sesame seeds, toasted
1 tsp honey
1 tsp sesame oil
1 tbsp hazelnut oil

1 ▼ Break the vermicelli into small strands. Heat a wok or frying pan (skillet) and dry-fry the vermicelli until lightly golden. Remove from the pan and set aside.

2 Shred the Chinese leaves and wash with the bean-sprouts. Drain thoroughly and place in a large bowl. Slice the radishes. Trim the mangetout (snow peas) and cut each into 3. Cut the carrot into thin matchsticks.

3 ▲ Add the sprouting beans and prepared vegetables to the bowl.

4 Place all the dressing ingredients in a screw-top jar and shake until well-blended. Pour over the salad and toss.

5 ▲ Transfer the salad to a serving bowl and sprinkle over the reserved vermicelli before serving.

CELERY & GREEN (BELL) PEPPER WITH SESAME DRESSING

This recipe makes a very elegant and light salad which will complement rice and noodle dishes beautifully.

SERVES 4

❁❁❁❁❁❁❁❁❁❁❁❁❁❁❁

INGREDIENTS:
125 g/4 oz/2 cups bean-sprouts
3 celery sticks, cut into 2.5 cm/1 inch
  pieces
1 large green (bell) pepper, chopped
1 large Granny Smith apple
2 tbsp sesame seeds to garnish

DRESSING:
1½ tbsp chopped coriander
  (cilantro)
3 tbsp fresh lime juice
½ tsp mild chilli powder
1 tsp sugar
½ tsp salt

❁❁❁❁❁❁❁❁❁❁❁❁❁❁❁

1 Rinse and drain the bean-sprouts. Pick them over and remove any that seem a little brown or limp – it is essential that they are fresh and crunchy for this recipe.

2 ▼ To make the dressing, combine the coriander (cilantro), lime juice, chilli powder, sugar and salt in a small bowl and mix thoroughly.

3 ▲ In a larger bowl, combine the celery, (bell) pepper, bean-sprouts and apple.

4 To prepare the garnish, toast the sesame seeds in a dry skillet until they are just turning colour.

5 ▲ Stir the dressing into the mixed vegetables just before serving. Garnish with the toasted sesame seeds.

CARROT & CORIANDER (CILANTRO) SALAD

This is a tangy, crunchy salad, which is popular with everyone. It makes an ideal accompaniment to many oriental main dishes.

SERVES 4

✻❁✻❁✻❁✻❁✻❁✻❁✻❁✻❁

INGREDIENTS:
4 large carrots
2 celery sticks, cut into matchsticks
2 tbsp roughly chopped fresh coriander
  (cilantro)

DRESSING:
1 tbsp sesame oil
1¼ tbsp rice vinegar
¼ tsp sugar
¼ tsp salt

✻❁✻❁✻❁✻❁✻❁✻❁✻❁✻❁✻

1 ▼ To create flower-shaped carrot slices, as shown, cut several grooves lengthways along each carrot before slicing it. Slice each carrot into very thin slices, using the slicing cutter of a grater.

2 ▼ Combine the carrot, celery and coriander (cilantro) in a bowl.

3 ▲ To make the dressing, combine the sesame oil, rice vinegar, sugar and salt thoroughly in a separate bowl.

4 ▼ Just before serving, toss the carrot, celery and coriander (cilantro) mixture in the dressing and transfer to a serving dish.

THAI SALAD

This is a typical Thai-style salad made by mixing fruit and vegetables with the sharp, sweet and fishy flavours of the dressing.

SERVES 4–6

INGREDIENTS:
250 g/8 oz white cabbage, finely
  shredded
2 tomatoes, skinned, deseeded and
  chopped
250 g/8 oz cooked French (green)
  beans, halved if large
125 g/4 oz peeled prawns (shrimp)
1 papaya, peeled, deseeded and
  chopped
1–2 red chillies, deseeded and very
  finely sliced
60 g/2 oz/scant ⅓ cup roasted salted
  peanuts, crushed
handful of lettuce or baby spinach
  leaves, shredded or torn into
  small pieces

DRESSING:
4 tbsp lime juice
2 tbsp Thai fish sauce
sugar, to taste
pepper
sprigs of coriander (cilantro),
  to garnish

1 ▼ Mix the cabbage with the tomatoes, French (green) beans, prawns (shrimp), three-quarters of the chopped papaya and half the sliced chillies in a large bowl. Stir in two-thirds of the crushed roasted peanuts and mix thoroughly.

2 ▼ Line the rim of a large serving plate with the lettuce or spinach and pile the salad mixture into the centre.

3 To make the dressing, beat the lime juice with the fish sauce and add sugar and pepper to taste. Drizzle the dressing over the salad.

4 ▼ Scatter the top with the remaining papaya, chillies and crushed peanuts. Garnish with coriander (cilantro) leaves and serve at once.

BRAISED CHINESE VEGETABLES

This dish is also known as Lo Han Zhai or Buddha's Delight. The original recipe calls for no less than 18 different vegetables to represent the 18 Buddhas (Lo Han).

SERVES 4

INGREDIENTS:
5 g/¼ oz dried wood ears
1 cake tofu (bean curd)
60 g/2 oz mangetout (snow peas)
125 g/4 oz Chinese leaves
1 small carrot
90 g/3 oz canned baby sweetcorn, drained
90 g/3 oz canned straw mushrooms, drained
60 g/2 oz canned water chestnuts, drained
300 ml/½ pint/1¼ cups vegetable oil
1 tsp salt
½ tsp sugar
1 tbsp light soy sauce or oyster sauce
2-3 tbsp chicken stock or water
a few drops of sesame oil

1 Soak the wood ears in warm water for 15–20 minutes, then rinse and drain, discarding any hard bits, and dry on paper towels.

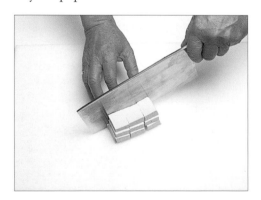

2 ▲ Cut the cake of tofu (bean curd) into about 18 small pieces. Top and tail the mangetout (snow peas). Cut the Chinese leaves and the carrot into slices roughly the same size and shape as the mangetout (snow peas). Cut the baby sweetcorn, the straw mushrooms and the water chestnuts in half.

3 ▼ Heat the oil in a preheated wok. Add the tofu (bean curd) and deep-fry for about 2 minutes until it turns slightly golden. Remove with a slotted spoon and drain on paper towels.

4 Pour off the oil, leaving about 2 tablespoons in the wok. Add the carrot, Chinese leaves and mangetout (snow peas) and stir-fry for 1 minute.

5 ▲ Now add the sweetcorn, mushrooms and water chestnuts. Stir gently for 2 more minutes, then add the salt, sugar, soy sauce and stock or water. Bring to the boil and stir-fry for 1 more minute.

6 Sprinkle the vegetables with a few drops of sesame oil and serve hot or cold.

SPINACH WITH STRAW MUSHROOMS

Straw mushrooms are available in cans from oriental shops. Here they are served with spinach, raisins and pine kernels (nuts). You can use button mushrooms instead, if straw mushrooms are unavailable.

SERVES 4

❀❀❀❀❀❀❀❀❀❀❀❀❀❀

INGREDIENTS:
30 g/1 oz/¼ cup pine kernels (nuts)
500 g/1 lb fresh spinach leaves
3 tbsp vegetable oil
1 red onion, sliced
2 garlic cloves, sliced
425 g/14 oz can of straw mushrooms,
*   drained*
30 g/1 oz/3 tbsp raisins
2 tbsp soy sauce
salt

❀❀❀❀❀❀❀❀❀❀❀❀❀❀

1 ▼ Heat a wok or large frying pan (skillet) and dry-fry the pine kernels (nuts) until lightly browned. Remove and set aside.

2 Wash the spinach thoroughly, picking the leaves over and removing long stalks. Drain and pat dry with paper towels.

3 ▲ Heat the oil in the wok or frying pan (skillet). Add the onion and garlic, and stir-fry for 1 minute.

4 ▼ Add the spinach and straw mushrooms, and continue to stir-fry until the leaves have wilted. Drain off any excess liquid.

5 Stir in the raisins, reserved pine kernels (nuts) and soy sauce. Stir-fry until thoroughly heated and well-mixed. Season to taste with salt before serving.

STIR-FRIED BEAN-SPROUTS

Be sure to use fresh bean-sprouts, rather than the canned variety, for this crunchy-textured dish.

SERVES 4

INGREDIENTS:
250 g/8 oz fresh bean-sprouts
2–3 spring onions (scallions)
1 medium fresh red chilli (optional)
3 tbsp vegetable oil
½ tsp salt
½ tsp sugar
1 tbsp light soy sauce
few drops of sesame oil (optional)

1 ▼ Rinse the bean-sprouts in cold water, discarding any husks or small pieces that float to the top. Drain well on paper towels.

2 ▼ Cut the spring onions (scallions) into short sections. Thinly shred the fresh red chilli, if using, discarding the seeds.

3 ▲ Heat the oil in a preheated wok. Add the bean-sprouts, spring onions (scallions) and shredded chilli, if using, and stir-fry for about 2 minutes.

4 ▼ Add the salt, sugar, soy sauce and sesame oil, if using, to the mixture in the wok. Stir well to blend. Serve hot or cold.

GOLDEN NEEDLES WITH BAMBOO SHOOTS

Golden needles are the dried flower buds of the tiger lily. They are usually sold in the dried form and can be obtained from specialist Chinese shops. They give a unique musky flavour to this dish.

SERVES 4

INGREDIENTS:

30 g/1 oz/¼ cup dried lily flowers
2 x 225 g/7½ oz cans of bamboo shoots, drained
60 g/2 oz/½ cup cornflour (cornstarch)
vegetable oil, for deep-frying
1 tbsp vegetable oil
450ml/¾ pint/scant 2 cups vegetable stock
1 tbsp dark soy sauce
1 tbsp dry sherry
1 tsp sugar
1 large garlic clove, sliced
¼ each red, green and yellow (bell) peppers

1 ▼ Soak the lily flowers in hot water for 30 minutes.

2 Coat the bamboo shoots in cornflour (cornstarch). Heat enough oil in a large heavy-based saucepan to deep-fry the bamboo shoots in batches until just beginning to colour. The oil should be 180–190°C/350–375°F, or hot enough so a bread cube browns in 30 seconds. Remove the bamboo shoots with a perforated spoon and drain on paper towels.

3 ▼ Drain the lily flowers and trim off the hard ends. Heat 1 tablespoon oil in a wok or large frying pan (skillet). Add the lily flowers, bamboo shoots, vegetable stock, soy sauce, sherry, sugar and garlic.

4 ▼ Slice the (bell) peppers thinly and add to the wok or pan (skillet). Bring to the boil, stirring constantly, then reduce the heat and simmer for 5 minutes. Add extra water or stock if necessary.

BROCCOLI IN OYSTER SAUCE

Some Cantonese restaurants use only the stalks of the broccoli for this dish, for added crunch. If the stalks are cut very thinly, they can be added to the pan at the same time as the florets.

SERVES 4

INGREDIENTS:
250–300 g/8–10 oz broccoli
3 tbsp vegetable oil
3–4 small slices ginger root
½ tsp salt
½ tsp sugar
3–4 tbsp chicken stock or water
1 tbsp oyster sauce

1 ▼ Cut the broccoli spears into small florets. Trim the stalks, peel off the rough skin, and cut the stalks diagonally into diamond shapes.

2 ▼ Heat the oil in a preheated wok and add the pieces of stalk and the ginger. Stir-fry for half a minute then add the florets and continue to stir-fry for another 2 minutes.

3 ▲ Add the salt, sugar and stock or water, and continue stirring for another minute or so.

4 ▼ Blend in the oyster sauce, stirring to coat the broccoli well. Serve hot or cold.

SWEET & SOUR VEGETABLES

Make your own choice of vegetables from the suggested list, including spring onions (scallions) and garlic. For a hotter, spicier sauce add chilli sauce.

SERVES 4

INGREDIENTS:
5–6 vegetables from the following:
1 (bell) pepper, red, green or yellow, cored, seeded and sliced
125 g/4 oz French (green) beans, cut into 2–3 pieces
125 g/4 oz mangetout (snow peas), cut into 2–3 pieces
250 g/8 oz green broccoli or cauliflower, divided into tiny florets
250 g/8 oz courgettes (zucchini), cut into thin 5 cm/2 inch lengths
175 g/6 oz carrots, cut into julienne strips
125 g/4 oz baby sweetcorn, sliced thinly
2 leeks, sliced thinly and cut into matchsticks
175 g/6 oz parsnip, finely diced
175 g/6 oz celeriac, finely diced
3 celery sticks, thinly sliced crosswise
4 tomatoes, skinned, quartered and seeded
125 g/4 oz button or closed-cup mushrooms, thinly sliced
7 cm/3 inch length of cucumber, diced
200 g/7 oz can water chestnuts or bamboo shoots, drained and sliced
425 g/15 oz can bean-sprouts or hearts of palm, drained and sliced
4 spring onions (scallions) trimmed and thinly sliced
1 garlic clove, crushed
2 tbsp sunflower oil

SWEET & SOUR SAUCE:
2 tbsp wine vinegar
2 tbsp clear honey
1 tbsp tomato purée (paste)
2 tbsp soy sauce
2 tbsp sherry
1–2 tsp sweet chilli sauce (optional)
2 tsp cornflour (cornstarch)

1 ▲ Prepare the selected vegetables, cutting them into uniform lengths.

2 ▼ Combine the sauce ingredients in a bowl, blending well together.

3 Heat the oil in the wok, swirling it around until really hot. Add the spring onions (scallions) and garlic and stir-fry for 1 minute.

4 ▼ Add the prepared vegetables – the harder ones first – and stir-fry for 2 minutes. Then add the softer mushrooms, mangetout (snow peas), tomatoes and stir-fry for 2 minutes.

5 ▼ Add the sauce and bring to the boil quickly, tossing all the vegetables until they are thoroughly coated and the sauce has thickened. Serve hot.

MIXED VEGETABLES IN COCONUT MILK

This is a deliciously crunchy way to prepare a mixture of vegetables.

SERVES 4-6

INGREDIENTS:
1 red chilli, deseeded and chopped
1 tsp coriander seeds
1 tsp cumin seeds
2 garlic cloves, crushed
1¼ tbsp lime juice
250 ml/8 fl oz/1 cup coconut milk
125 g/4 oz/2 cups bean-sprouts
125 g/4 oz/2 cups white cabbage, shredded
125 g/4 oz mangetout (snow peas), trimmed
125 g/4 oz/1¼ cups carrots, sliced thinly
125 g/4 oz/1¼ cups cauliflower florets
3 tbsp peanut butter
grated or shaved coconut, to garnish

1 Grind together the chilli, coriander and cumin seeds, garlic and lime juice in a pestle and mortar, spice grinder or food processor.

2 ▼ Put the spices into a medium saucepan and heat gently until fragrant, about 1 minute. Add the coconut milk and stir until just about to boil.

3 ▼ Meanwhile, mix all the prepared vegetables together in a large bowl.

4 ▲ Stir the peanut butter into the coconut mixture and combine with the vegetables. Sprinkle over the grated or shaved coconut and serve immediately.

MEAT & POULTRY DISHES

Included in this chapter is a delectable range of chicken, duck, beef and pork dishes, from familiar oriental favourites like Lemon Chicken and Aromatic & Crispy Duck through Japanese-inspired sukiyaki and teriyaki dishes to Thai green curries. Some of the dishes, such as the Thai-flavoured Roast Baby Chickens, are adapted slightly for Westerners but have all the exotic flavour of the East. You will find many different cooking techniques used throughout this chapter. Beef can be cooked by various methods, and one of the favourites is stir-frying which gives the meat a slightly dry, chewy texture. Braising and steaming are popular Szechuan methods of cooking beef and pork, and this method results in tender meat. Double-cooking also results in succulent meat; here the meat is first tenderized by a long slow simmering in water, followed by a quick crisping or stir-frying in a sauce – Twice-Cooked Pork is a delicious example of this technique.

BEEF & BOK CHOY (PAGE 68)

SUKIYAKI BEEF

An easy way of giving beef a Japanese flavour is to marinate the meat in teriyaki sauce and sherry: it can be left for anything from 1–24 hours. Hearts of palm and mushrooms blend well with the beef.

SERVES 4

INGREDIENTS:

2.5 cm/1 inch ginger root, grated
1 garlic clove, crushed
4 tbsp sherry
4 tbsp teriyaki sauce
500–625 g/1–1¼ lb sirloin, rump or
  fillet steak
425 g/15 oz can hearts of palm
2 tbsp sesame or sunflower oil
125 g/4 oz button or closed-cup
  mushrooms, thinly sliced
salt and pepper

TO GARNISH:

sesame seeds (optional)
spring onion (scallion) tassles

1 Blend the ginger in a shallow dish with the garlic, sherry and teriyaki sauce, adding a little salt.

2 ▼ Cut the steak into narrow strips about 2.5–4 cm/1–1½ inches long, across the grain. Add the strips to the marinade in the dish, mix thoroughly to coat, cover and leave in a cool place for at least 1 hour and up to 24 hours.

3 Drain the hearts of palm and cut into slanting slices about 1 cm/½ inch thick.

4 ▼ Remove the beef from the marinade with a slotted spoon, reserving the marinade. Heat the oil in the wok, swirling it around until it is really hot. Add the beef and stir-fry for 2 minutes, then add the mushrooms and continue to cook for a further minute.

5 ▲ Add the hearts of palm to the wok with the reserved marinade and stir-fry for another minute, making sure the meat is thoroughly coated in the sauce. Adjust the seasoning and serve sprinkled with sesame seeds, if using, and garnished with spring onion (scallion) tassles.

BEEF WITH BEANS

Strips of steak with a strong flavouring of sherry, teriyaki sauce and orange make this an ideal dish for entertaining.

SERVES 4

INGREDIENTS:
500–625 g/1–1¼ lb sirloin, rump or
    fillet steak
1 orange
2 tbsp sesame oil
4 spring onions (scallions), thinly sliced
    diagonally
175 g/6 oz French or fine (green)
    beans, cut into 2–3 pieces
1 garlic clove, crushed
4 tbsp sherry
1½ tbsp teriyaki sauce
¼ tsp ground allspice
1 tsp sugar
425 g/15 oz can cannellini beans,
    drained
salt and pepper

TO GARNISH:
orange slices
fresh bay leaves

1 Cut the steak into narrow strips, about 4 cm/1½ inches long, cutting across the grain.

2 ▲ Remove the rind from the orange using a citrus zester or canelle knife (citrus stripper), or pare thinly with a potato peeler, and cut the rind into julienne strips. Squeeze the orange and reserve the juice.

3 ▲ Heat 1 tablespoon of the oil in a wok or large frying pan (skillet). Add the strips of beef and stir-fry briskly for about 2 minutes, then remove from the wok and keep warm.

4 Add the remaining oil and when hot add the spring onions (scallions) and garlic and stir-fry for 1–2 minutes. Add the French (green) beans and continue to cook for 2 minutes.

5 ▼ Add the sherry, teriyaki, orange rind and 3 tablespoons of orange juice, allspice, sugar and seasoning and when well mixed return the beef and any juices to the wok.

6 Stir-fry for 1–2 minutes, then add the cannellini beans and stir until piping hot. Adjust the seasoning. Serve garnished with orange slices and bay leaves.

BEEF & BOK CHOY

A colourful selection of vegetables are stir-fried with tender strips of steak.

SERVES 4

❀❀❀❀❀❀❀❀❀❀❀❀❀❀❀❀

INGREDIENTS:
*1 large head of bok choy, about
    250–275 g/8–9 oz, roughly torn
2 tbsp vegetable oil
2 garlic cloves, crushed
500 g/1 lb rump or fillet steak, cut into
    thin strips
150 g/5 oz mangetout (snow peas),
    trimmed
150 g/5 oz baby sweetcorn
6 spring onions (scallions), chopped
2 red (bell) peppers, cored, deseeded
    and thinly sliced
2 tbsp oyster sauce
1 tbsp Thai fish sauce
1 tbsp sugar*

❀❀❀❀❀❀❀❀❀❀❀❀❀❀❀❀

1 ▼ Steam the bok choy leaves
over boiling water until just tender.
Keep warm.

2 ▼ Heat the oil in a large,
heavy-based frying pan (skillet) or

wok, add the garlic and beef strips and
stir-fry until just browned, about
1–2 minutes.

3 ▲ Add the mangetout (snow peas),
baby sweetcorn, spring onions
(scallions), red (bell) pepper, oyster
sauce, fish sauce and sugar to the pan
(skillet) or wok.

4 ▼ Mix well and stir-fry for a further
2–3 minutes until the vegetables are
just tender, but still crisp.

5 Arrange the bok choy leaves in the
base of a heated serving dish and
spoon the beef and vegetable mixture
into the centre. Serve immediately,
with rice or noodles.

BEEF & CHILLI BLACK BEAN SAUCE

It is not necessary to use the expensive cuts of beef steak for this recipe: the meat will be tender, as it is cut into small thin slices and marinated.

SERVES 4

INGREDIENTS:
250–300 g/8–10 oz beef steak
 (such as rump)
1 small onion
1 small green (bell) pepper, cored and
 deseeded
about 300 ml/½ pint/1¼ cups vegetable
 oil
1 spring onion (scallion), cut into short
 sections
few small slices of fresh ginger root
1–2 small green or red chillies,
 deseeded and sliced
2 tbsp crushed black bean sauce

MARINADE:
¼ tsp bicarbonate of soda (baking soda)
 or baking powder
¼ tsp sugar
1 tbsp light soy sauce
2 tsp Chinese rice wine or dry sherry
2 tsp cornflour (cornstarch) paste
 (see page 15)
2 tsp sesame oil

1 ▼ Cut the beef into small thin strips. Mix together the marinade ingredients in a shallow dish, add the beef strips, turn to coat and leave to marinate for at least 2–3 hours – the longer the better.

2 Cut the onion and green (bell) pepper into small cubes.

3 ▼ Heat the oil in a preheated wok, or in a frying pan (skillet). Add the beef strips and stir-fry for about 1 minute, or until the colour changes. Remove the beef strips from the oil with a slotted spoon and drain on paper towels. Keep warm.

4 ▲ Pour off the excess oil, leaving about 1 tablespoon in the wok or pan (skillet). Add the spring onion (scallion), ginger, chillies, onion and green (bell) pepper and stir-fry for about 1 minute. Add the black bean sauce, stir until smooth, then return the beef strips to the wok or pan. Blend well and stir-fry for another minute. Serve hot.

GREEN CHILLI CHICKEN

The green chilli paste gives a hot and spicy flavour to the chicken, which takes on a vibrant green colour.

SERVES 4

❋❋❋❋❋❋❋❋❋❋❋❋❋❋❋❋❋

INGREDIENTS:
5 tbsp vegetable oil
500 g/1 lb boneless chicken breasts, sliced into thin strips
50 ml/2 fl oz/¼ cup coconut milk
3 tbsp brown sugar
3 tsp fish sauce
3 tbsp sliced red and green chillies, seeded
4-6 tbsp chopped fresh basil
3 tbsp thick coconut milk or cream
finely chopped fresh chillies, deseeded, lemon grass and lemon slices, to garnish

GREEN CURRY PASTE:
2 tsp ground ginger
2 tsp ground coriander
2 tsp caraway seeds,
2 tsp ground nutmeg
2 tsp shrimp paste
2 tsp salt
2 tsp black pepper
pinch of ground cloves
1 stalk lemon grass, finely chopped
2 tbsp chopped coriander
2 garlic cloves, peeled
2 onions, peeled
grated rind and juice of 2 limes
4 fresh green chillies, about 5 cm/ 2 inches long, deseeded

❋❋❋❋❋❋❋❋❋❋❋❋❋❋❋❋❋

1 To make the curry paste, place all the ingredients and 2 tablespoons of the oil in a food processor or blender and process to a smooth paste.

2 Heat the remaining oil in a heavy-based pan or wok. Add the curry paste and cook for about 30 seconds.

3 ▼ Add the chicken strips to the wok and stir-fry over a high heat for about 2–3 minutes.

4 Add the coconut milk, brown sugar, fish sauce and chillies. Cook for 5 minutes, stirring frequently.

5 ▲ Remove from the heat, add the basil and toss well to mix.

6 Transfer the chicken to a warmed serving dish. To serve, spoon on a little of the thick coconut milk or cream and garnish with chopped chillies, lemon grass and lemon slices. Serve with steamed or boiled rice.
Sprinkle with chopped basil and serve accompanied with rice.

PEPPERED BEEF CASHEWS

A simple but stunning dish of tender strips of beef mixed with crunchy cashew nuts, coated in a hot sauce. Serve with rice noodles.

SERVES 6

✿✿✿✿✿✿✿✿✿✿✿✿✿✿✿✿✿✿✿✿✿

INGREDIENTS:
1 tbsp groundnut or sunflower oil
1 tbsp sesame oil
1 onion, sliced
1 garlic clove, crushed
1 tbsp grated ginger root
500 g/1 lb fillet or rump steak, cut into thin strips
2 tsp palm or demerara sugar
2 tbsp light soy sauce
1 small yellow (bell) pepper, cored, seeded and sliced
1 red (bell) pepper, cored, seeded and sliced
4 spring onions (scallions), chopped
2 celery sticks, chopped
4 large open-cap mushrooms, sliced
4 tbsp roasted cashew nuts
3 tbsp stock or white wine

✿✿✿✿✿✿✿✿✿✿✿✿✿✿✿✿✿✿✿✿✿

2 ▲ Add the steak strips and stir-fry for a further 2–3 minutes, until the meat has browned. Add the sugar and soy sauce, mixing well.

4 Add the (bell) peppers, spring onions (scallions), celery, mushrooms and cashews, mixing well.

5 ▼ Add the stock or wine and stir-fry for 2–3 minutes until the beef is cooked through and the vegetables are tender-crisp.

6 Serve the stir-fry immediately with rice noodles.

1 ▲ Heat the oils in a large, heavy-based frying pan or wok. Add the onion, garlic and ginger and stir-fry for about 2 minutes until softened and lightly coloured.

LEMON CHICKEN

Lemon sauce is a easily available from oriental stores, or you can make your own. It is a Cantonese speciality.

SERVES 4

INGREDIENTS:
*350 g/12 oz chicken breast fillets,
    skinned
1 tbsp Chinese rice wine or dry sherry
1 egg, beaten
4 tbsp plain (all-purpose) flour blended
    with 2 tbsp water
vegetable oil, for deep-frying
homemade sauce (see below), or
    ready-made lemon sauce
salt and pepper
slices of fresh lemon, to garnish
plain boiled rice, to serve (optional)*

LEMON SAUCE:
*1 tbsp vegetable oil
250 ml/8 fl oz/1 cup chicken stock
1 tbsp caster (superfine) sugar
1 tbsp lemon juice
1 tbsp cornflour (cornstarch)
1 tsp salt
1 tsp grated lemon rind*

1 To make the lemon sauce, heat the oil in a wok or saucepan until hot, reduce the heat and add all the other sauce ingredients. Blend well, then bring to the boil and stir until smooth.

2 ▲ Cut the chicken into thin slices and place in a shallow dish with wine, salt and pepper. Leave to marinate for 25–30 minutes.

3 Make a batter by mixing together the beaten egg and the flour paste. Place the chicken slices in the batter and turn to coat well.

4 ▲ Heat the oil in a wok or deep-fat fryer to 180-190°C/350–375°F, or until a cube of bread browns in 30 seconds. Deep-fry the chicken slices until golden brown, then remove

with a slotted spoon and drain on paper towels. Cut the chicken slices into bite-sized pieces.

5 ▼ Heat about 1 tablespoon of oil in a wok or pan. Stir in the prepared lemon sauce until well blended and pour evenly over the chicken. Garnish with lemon slices and serve with rice, if wished.

PEANUT SESAME CHICKEN

In this quickly prepared dish chicken strips are stir-fried with vegetables. Sesame and peanuts give extra crunch and flavour and the fruit juice glaze gives a lovely shiny coating to the sauce.

SERVES 4

INGREDIENTS:
2 tbsp vegetable oil
2 tbsp sesame oil
500g/1 lb boneless, skinned chicken
    breasts, sliced into strips
250 g/8 oz broccoli, divided into small
    florets
250 g/8 oz baby sweetcorn, halved
    if large
1 small red (bell) pepper, cored,
    deseeded and sliced
2 tbsp soy sauce
250 ml/8 fl oz/1 cup orange juice
2 tsp cornflour (cornstarch)
2 tbsp toasted sesame seeds
60 g/2 oz/⅓ cup roasted, shelled,
    unsalted peanuts
rice or noodles, to serve

1 Heat the oils in a large, heavy-based frying pan (skillet) or wok, add the chicken strips and stir-fry until browned, about 4–5 minutes.

2 ▲ Add the broccoli, sweetcorn and red (bell) pepper and stir-fry for a further 1–2 minutes.

3 ▼ Meanwhile, mix the soy sauce with the orange juice and cornflour (cornstarch). Stir into the chicken and vegetable mixture, stirring constantly until the sauce has slightly thickened and a glaze develops.

4 ▼ Stir in the toasted sesame seeds and roasted peanuts, mixing well. Heat for a further 3–4 minutes, then serve at once, with rice or noodles.

CHICKEN WITH BEAN-SPROUTS

This is the basic chicken chop suey to be found in almost every Chinese restaurant in the world.

SERVES 4

INGREDIENTS:
125 g/4 oz chicken breast fillet, skinned
1 tsp salt
¼ egg white, lightly beaten
2 tsp cornflour (cornstarch) paste (see page 15)
about 300 ml/½ pint/1¼ cups vegetable oil
1 small onion, thinly shredded
1 small green (bell) pepper, cored, deseeded and thinly shredded
1 small carrot, thinly shredded
125 g/4 oz fresh bean-sprouts
½ tsp sugar
1 tbsp light soy sauce
1 tsp Chinese rice wine or dry sherry
2–3 tbsp Chinese Stock (see page 10)
few drops of sesame oil
chilli sauce, to serve

1 Thinly shred the chicken and mix with a pinch of the salt, the egg white and cornflour (cornstarch) paste.

2 ▲ Heat the oil in a preheated wok, or large frying pan (skillet), and stir-fry the chicken for about 1 minute, stirring to separate the shreds. Remove with a slotted spoon and drain on paper towels.

3 ▼ Pour off the oil, leaving about 2 tablespoons in the wok. Add all the vegetables except the bean-sprouts and stir-fry for about 2 minutes, then add the bean-sprouts and stir for a few more seconds.

4 ▲ Add the chicken with the remaining salt, sugar, soy sauce and wine, blend well and add the stock or water. Sprinkle with the sesame oil and serve at once, accompanied by the chilli sauce.

KUNG PO CHICKEN WITH CASHEW NUTS

Peanuts, walnuts or almonds can be used instead of the cashew nuts, if preferred.

SERVES 4

❋❋❋❋❋❋❋❋❋❋❋❋❋❋❋❋❋❋

INGREDIENTS:
250–300 g/8–10 oz chicken meat, boned and skinned
¼ tsp salt
¼ egg white
1 tsp cornflour (cornstarch) paste (see page 15)
1 medium green (bell) pepper, cored and deseeded
4 tbsp vegetable oil
1 spring onion (scallion), cut into short sections
few small slices of ginger root
4–5 small dried red chillies, soaked, deseeded and shredded
2 tbsp crushed yellow bean sauce
1 tsp Chinese rice wine or dry sherry
125 g/4 oz roasted cashew nuts
few drops of sesame oil
plain boiled rice, to serve

❋❋❋❋❋❋❋❋❋❋❋❋❋❋❋❋❋❋

1 ▼ Cut the chicken into small cubes about the size of sugar lumps. Place the chicken in a small bowl and mix with a pinch of salt, the egg white and the cornflour (cornstarch) paste, in that order.

2 Cut the green (bell) pepper into cubes or triangles about the same size as the chicken pieces.

3 ▼ Heat the oil in a preheated wok, or frying pan (skillet), add the chicken cubes and stir-fry for about 1 minute, or until the colour changes. Remove with a slotted spoon and keep warm.

4 Add the spring onion (scallion), ginger, chillies and green (bell) pepper. Stir-fry for about 1 minute.

5 ▼ Add the chicken with the yellow bean sauce and wine. Blend well and stir-fry for another minute. Finally stir in the cashew nuts and sesame oil. Serve hot with rice.

ROAST BABY CHICKENS

Baby chickens, stuffed with lemon grass and lime leaves, coated with a spicy Thai paste, then roasted until crisp and golden, make a wonderful, aromatic dish for a special occasion.

SERVES 4

INGREDIENTS:
*4 small baby chickens, weighing about 350–500 g/12 oz–1 lb each
mixed wild and basmati rice, to serve*

TO GARNISH:
*coriander (cilantro) leaves
lime wedges*

MARINADE:
*4 garlic cloves, peeled
2 fresh coriander (cilantro) roots
1 tbsp light soy sauce
salt and pepper*

STUFFING:
*4 stalks lemon grass
4 kaffir lime leaves
4 slices ginger root
about 6 tbsp coconut milk, to brush*

1 Wash the chickens and pat dry with paper towels.

2 ▲ Place all the ingredients for the marinade in a blender and process until smooth, or grind down in a pestle and mortar. Season to taste with salt and pepper. Rub this marinade mixture into the skin of the chickens, using the back of a spoon to spread it evenly over the skins.

3 Place a stalk of lemon grass, a lime leaf and a piece of ginger in the cavity of each chicken.

4 ▼ Place the chickens in a roasting tin (pan) and brush lightly with the coconut milk. Roast for 30 minutes in a preheated oven at 200°C/400°F/Gas Mark 6.

5 Remove from the oven and brush again with coconut milk.

6 ▼ Return the chicken to the oven and cook for a further 15–25 minutes, until golden and cooked through; depending upon the size of the chickens. The chickens are cooked when the juices from the thigh run clear when pricked with are sharp knife and are not tinged at all with pink.

7 Serve with the pan juices poured over. Garnish with coriander (cilantro) leaves and lime wedges.

AROMATIC & CRISPY DUCK

Although the pancakes traditionally served with this dish are not too difficult to make, the process is very time-consuming. Buy ready-made ones from oriental stores, or use crisp lettuce leaves as the wrapper.

SERVES 4

INGREDIENTS:
2 large duckling quarters
1 tsp salt
3–4 pieces star anise
1 tsp Szechuan red peppercorns
1 tsp cloves
2 cinnamon sticks, broken into pieces
2–3 spring onions (scallions), cut into
  short sections
4–5 small slices ginger root
3–4 tbsp Chinese rice wine or dry
  sherry
vegetable oil, for deep-frying

TO SERVE:
12 ready-made pancakes or 12 crisp
  lettuce leaves
hoisin or plum sauce
‡ cucumber, thinly shredded
3–4 spring onions (scallions), thinly
  shredded

1 ▲ Rub the duck pieces with the salt and arrange the star anise, peppercorns, cloves and cinnamon on top. Sprinkle with the spring onions (scallions), ginger and rice wine or sherry and leave to marinate for at least 3–4 hours.

2 ▼ Arrange the duck pieces (with the marinade spices) on a plate that will fit inside a bamboo steamer. Pour some hot water into a wok, place the bamboo steamer in the wok, sitting on a trivet. Put in the duck and cover with the bamboo lid. Steam the duck pieces (with the marinade) over high heat for at least 2–3 hours, until tender and cooked through. Top up the hot water from time to time as required.

3 Remove the duck and leave to cool for at least 4–5 hours – this is very important; unless the duck is cold and dry, it will not be crispy.

4 ▲ Pour off the water and wipe the wok dry. Pour in the oil and heat until smoking. Deep-fry the duck pieces, skin-side down, for 4–5 minutes or until crisp and brown. Remove and drain on paper towels.

5 To serve, scrape the meat off the bone, place about 1 teaspoon of hoisin or plum sauce on the centre of a pancake (or lettuce leaf), add a few pieces of cucumber and spring onion (scallion) with a portion of the duck meat. Wrap up to form a small parcel and eat with your fingers. Provide plenty of paper napkins for your guests.

DUCK WITH GINGER & LIME

Just the thing for a lazy summer day – roasted duck breasts sliced and served with a dressing made of ginger, lime juice, sesame oil and fish sauce. Serve on a bed of assorted fresh salad leaves.

SERVES 6

INGREDIENTS:
*3 boneless Barbary duck breasts, about 250 g/8 oz each
salt*

DRESSING:
*125 ml/4 fl oz/½ cup olive oil
2 tsp sesame oil
2 tbsp lime juice
grated rind and juice of 1 orange
2 tsp Thai fish sauce
1 tbsp grated ginger root
1 garlic clove, crushed
2 tsp light soy sauce
3 spring onions (scallions), finely chopped
1 tsp sugar
about 250 g/8 oz assorted salad leaves
orange slices, to garnish (optional)*

1 ▼ Wash the duck breasts, dry on paper towels, then cut in half. Prick the skin all over with a fork and season well with salt.

2 Place the duck pieces, skin-side down, on a wire rack or trivet over a roasting tin (pan). Cook the duck in the preheated oven at 200°C/400°F/Gas Mark 6 for 10 minutes.

3 Turn over and cook for a further 12–15 minutes, or until the duck is cooked, but still pink in the centre, and the skin is crisp.

4 ▼ To make the dressing, beat the oils with the lime juice, orange rind and juice, fish sauce, ginger, garlic, soy sauce, spring onions (scallions) and sugar until well blended.

5 ▼ Remove the duck from the oven, allow to cool, then cut into thick slices. Add a little of the dressing to moisten and coat the duck.

6 To serve, arrange salad leaves on a serving dish. Top with the sliced duck breasts and drizzle with the remaining salad dressing. Garnish with orange slices, if using, and serve at once.

DUCK WITH PINEAPPLE

For best results, use the cooked duck available from Chinese restaurants. Red wine vinegar can be substituted for the rice vinegar in the recipe.

SERVES 4

INGREDIENTS:
125–175 g/4–6 oz cooked duck meat
3 tbsp vegetable oil
1 small onion, thinly shredded
2–3 slices ginger root, thinly shredded
1 spring onion (scallion), thinly shredded
1 small carrot, thinly shredded
125 g/4 oz canned pineapple, cut into
   small slices
¼ tsp salt
1 tbsp red rice vinegar
2 tbsp syrup from the pineapple
1 tbsp cornflour (cornstarch) paste
   (see page 15)
black bean sauce, to serve (optional)

1 ▲ Cut the cooked duck into strips.

2 ▼ Heat the oil in a preheated wok, add the shredded onion and stir-fry until opaque.

3 Add the ginger, spring onion (scallion) and carrot shreds. Stir-fry for about 1 minute.

4 ▲ Add the duck and pineapple to with the salt, vinegar and pineapple syrup. Stir until well blended.

5 ▼ Add the cornflour (cornstarch) paste and stir for 1–2 minutes until the sauce has thickened. Serve hot with the black bean sauce, if using.

SPARE RIBS WITH CHILLI

For best results, chop the spare ribs into small bite-size pieces.

SERVES 4

❀❀❀❀❀❀❀❀❀❀❀❀❀❀❀❀

INGREDIENTS:

500 g/1 lb pork spare ribs
1 tsp sugar
1 tbsp light soy sauce
1 tsp Chinese rice wine or dry sherry
1 tsp cornflour (cornstarch)
about 600 ml/1pint/2½ cups vegetable oil
1 garlic clove, finely chopped
1 spring onion (scallion), cut into short pieces
1 small red or green chilli, thinly sliced
2 tbsp black bean sauce
about 150 ml/¼ pint/⅔ cup Chinese Stock (see page 10) or water
1 small onion, diced
1 medium green (bell) pepper, cored, deseeded and diced

❀❀❀❀❀❀❀❀❀❀❀❀❀❀❀❀

1 ▲ Trim excess fat from the ribs, and chop each one into 3–4 bite-sized pieces. Place the ribs in a shallow dish with the sugar, soy sauce, rice wine and cornflour (cornstarch) and leave to marinate for 35–45 minutes.

2 ▼ Heat the oil in a preheated wok until a bread cube browns in 30 seconds. Add the spare ribs and deep-fry for 2–3 minutes until light brown. Remove with a slotted spoon and drain on paper towels.

3 Pour off the oil, leaving 1 tablespoon in the wok. Add the garlic, spring onion (scallion), chilli and black bean sauce and stir-fry for 30–40 seconds.

4 Add the spare ribs, blend well, then add the stock or water. Bring to the boil, then reduce the heat, cover and braise for 8–10 minutes, stirring once or twice.

5 ▼ Add the onion and green (bell) pepper to the wok, increase the heat to high, and stir uncovered for about 2 minutes to reduce the sauce a little. Serve hot.

SWEET & SOUR PORK RIBS

Spare ribs, the traditional Chinese-style rib, have been used here. Baby back and loin ribs are also suitable.

SERVES 4–6

INGREDIENTS:
2 garlic cloves, crushed
5 cm/2 inch piece ginger, peeled and
   grated
150 ml/¼ pint/⅔ cup soy sauce
2 tbsp sugar
4 tbsp sweet sherry
4 tbsp tomato purée (paste)
300 g/10 oz/2 cups pineapple, cubed
2 kg/4 lb pork spare ribs
3 tbsp clear honey
300 g/10 oz/5 pineapple rings, fresh or
   canned

1 ▼ Combine the garlic, ginger, soy sauce, sugar, sherry, tomato purée (paste) and cubed pineapple in a non-porous dish.

2 ▼ Put the spare ribs into the dish and make sure that they are coated completely with the marinade. Cover the dish.

3 Leave at room temperature for 2 hours only.

4 ▲ Cook the ribs over a medium barbecue (grill) for 30–40 minutes, brushing with the honey after 20–30 minutes. Baste frequently with the reserved marinade until cooked.

5 ▲ Cook the pineapple rings over the barbecue (grill) for 10 minutes, turning once.

6 Serve the ribs with the charred pineapple rings on the side.

TWICE-COOKED PORK

Twice-cooked is a popular way of cooking meat in China. The meat is first boiled to tenderize it, then cut into strips or slices and stir-fried.

SERVES 4

❁❁❁❁❁❁❁❁❁❁❁❁❁❁

INGREDIENTS:

250–300 g/8–10 oz shoulder or leg of
  pork, in one piece
1 small green (bell) pepper, cored and
  deseeded
1 small red (bell) pepper, cored and
  deseeded
125 g/4 oz canned sliced bamboo
  shoots, rinsed and drained
3 tbsp vegetable oil
1 spring onion (scallion), cut into short
  pieces
1 tsp salt
¼ tsp sugar
1 tbsp light soy sauce
1 tsp chilli bean sauce or freshly minced
  chilli
1 tsp Chinese rice wine or dry sherry
few drops of sesame oil

❁❁❁❁❁❁❁❁❁❁❁❁❁❁

1 ▲ Immerse the pork in a saucepan of boiling water to cover. Return to the boil and skim the surface. Reduce the heat, cover and simmer for 15–20 minutes. Turn off the heat and leave the pork in the water to cool for at least 2–3 hours.

2 ▼ Remove the pork from the water and drain well. Trim off any excess fat, then cut into small, thin slices. Cut the green and red (bell) peppers into pieces about the same size as the pork and the sliced bamboo shoots.

3 Heat the oil in a preheated wok or frying pan (skillet) and add the vegetables and spring onion (scallion). Stir-fry for about 1 minute.

4 ▼ Add the pork, followed by the salt, sugar, soy sauce, chilli bean sauce and rice wine or sherry. Blend well, continue stirring for another minute, then sprinkle with a few drops of sesame oil and serve.

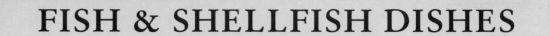

FISH & SHELLFISH DISHES

It is not surprising that fish and shellfish are such popular ingredients in Eastern cuisine, as there are many wonderful edible treasures to be found in the Pacific Ocean. In this chapter you will find recipes for white fish, monkfish, salmon, squid, scallops and prawns (shrimp). When choosing seafood, make sure it is absolutely fresh. Look for whole fish that have bright eyes, firm flesh, shiny scales and a fresh sea-like odour. Likewise choose shellfish that are still tightly locked and closed in their shells, discarding any that are already open.

Fish and shellfish can be cooked in various ways, but stir-frying and grilling (broiling) or barbecuing are popular methods. In Thailand whole fish are often steamed, fried, grilled (broiled) or baked, skewers of prawns (shrimp) and scallops are barbecued, and fish and seafood are stir-fried or made into curries with subtle yet mouth-watering flavours. Thai fish dishes sometimes include fruit, such as pineapple, papaya and mango. Many marinades and stir-fry sauces, such as black bean, sweet and sour or a spicy Szechuan sauce, can be used interchangeably with other fish and shellfish, and you may like to adapt the recipes on the following pages to suit your own tastes.

THAI PRAWN (SHRIMP) STIR-FRY (PAGE 90)

ORIENTAL MONKFISH TAIL WITH SWEET & SOUR VEGETABLES

Use a two-layered steamer for this recipe so you can cook the fish in one layer and the vegetables in the other. This fish dish is very low in fat.

SERVES 6

INGREDIENTS:
750 g/1½ lb monkfish tail
175 g/6 oz peeled prawns (shrimp), defrosted if frozen
4 spring onions (scallions), chopped
1 red chilli, deseeded and finely chopped
2 tbsp oyster sauce
175 g/6 oz/6 slices lean rindless back (Canadian) bacon

SWEET & SOUR VEGETABLES:
250 g/8 oz/2 courgettes (zucchini), trimmed
250 g/8 oz/2–3 carrots, peeled
1 red (bell) pepper, deseeded
125 g/4 oz/1⅓ cups mangetout (snow peas), trimmed
½ tsp grated lemon rind

SAUCE:
300 ml/½ pint/1¼ cups fish stock
4 tbsp white wine vinegar
1 tbsp caster (superfine) sugar
2 tbsp tomato purée (paste)
2 tbsp light soy sauce
2 tsp cornflour (cornstarch) mixed with 4 tsp cold water

1 ▼ Strip away the skin and membrane from the monkfish. Slice in half by cutting along the sides of the central bone.

2 Lay the fish between 2 layers of baking parchment and flatten to 1 cm/½ inch thick with a rolling pin.

3 Mix the remaining ingredients, except the bacon, to form a stuffing.

4 ▼ Press stuffing on to one half of the fish and top with the other piece. Lay 5 slices of bacon on baking parchment and place the fish on top. Fold the bacon over the fish and cover with the remaining bacon slices. Secure the fish layers with string.

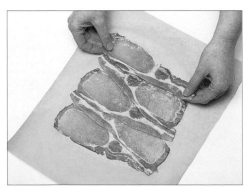

5 Place the fish into 1 compartment of a large steamer. Bring a wok or large pan of water to the boil and put the steamer on top. Cover and steam for 20 minutes.

6 ▲ Meanwhile slice the vegetables, except the mangetout (snow peas). Place in the second steaming compartment with the mangetout (snow peas) and lemon rind. Turn the fish over and place the vegetable compartment on top. Steam for 10 minutes until cooked.

7 To make sauce, put the ingredients into a pan. Bring to the boil, stirring, and simmer for 5 minutes. Slice the fish and serve with the sweet and sour vegetables and sauce.

BRAISED FISH FILLETS

Any white fish such as lemon sole or plaice is ideal for this dish.

SERVES 4

INGREDIENTS:

3–4 small Chinese dried mushrooms
300–350 g/10–12 oz white fish fillets
½ egg white, lightly beaten
1 tsp cornflour (cornstarch) paste
    (see page 15)
600 ml/1 pint/2½ cups vegetable oil
1 tsp finely chopped ginger root
2 spring onions (scallions), chopped
1 garlic clove, finely chopped
½ small green (bell) pepper, cored,
    deseeded and cut into small cubes
½ small carrot, thinly sliced
60 g/2 oz canned sliced bamboo shoots,
    rinsed and drained
1 tsp salt
½ tsp sugar
1 tbsp light soy sauce
1 tsp Chinese rice wine or dry sherry
1 tbsp chilli bean sauce
2–3 tbsp Chinese Stock (see page 10) or
    water
few drops of sesame oil
plain boiled rice, to serve

1 Soak the Chinese mushrooms in warm water for 30 minutes, then drain on paper towels, reserving the soaking water for stock or soup. Squeeze the mushrooms to extract all the moisture, cut off and discard any hard stems and slice the mushrooms thinly.

2 ▲ Cut the fish fillets into bite-sized pieces.

3 Then place in a shallow dish and mix with a pinch of salt, the egg white and cornflour (cornstarch) paste, turning the fish pieces to coat well.

4 ▼ Heat the oil to a temperature of 180–190°C/350–375°F, or until a cube of bread browns in 30 seconds. Deep-fry the fish pieces for about 1 minute. Remove with a slotted spoon and drain on paper towels.

5 Pour off the oil, leaving about 1 tablespoon in the wok. Add the

ginger, spring onions (scallions) and garlic to flavour the oil for a few seconds. Add the (bell) pepper, carrot and bamboo shoots and stir-fry for about 1 minute.

6 ▼ Add the sugar, soy sauce, rice wine, chilli bean sauce and stock or water and bring to the boil. Add the fish pieces, stir to coat well with the sauce, and braise for another minute.

7 Sprinkle with sesame oil and serve immediately with rice.

PINEAPPLE & FISH CURRY

This is a fiery hot Thai curry dish all the better for serving with refreshing (and cooling) fresh pineapple pieces.

SERVES 4

INGREDIENTS:
2 pineapples
7 cm/3 inch piece galangal, peeled and sliced
2 stalks lemon grass, bruised and chopped
5 sprigs fresh basil
500 g/1 lb firm white fish fillets, such as monkfish, halibut or cod, cubed
125 g/4 oz peeled prawns (shrimp)
2 tbsp vegetable oil
2 tbsp bottled Thai red curry paste
125 ml/4 fl oz/½ cup thick coconut milk or cream
2 tbsp Thai fish sauce
2 tsp palm or demerara sugar
2–3 red chillies, deseeded and cut into thin julienne strips
about 6 kaffir lime leaves, torn into pieces
sprigs of coriander (cilantro), to garnish

1 ▼ Cut the pineapples in half lengthways. Remove the flesh, reserving the hollowed-out shells for serving if wished. Remove the core from the pineapple flesh, then dice into bite-sized pieces.

2 Place the galangal in a large shallow pan with the lemon grass and basil. Add the fish cubes and just enough water to cover. Bring to the boil, reduce the heat and simmer for about 2 minutes.

3 ▼ Add the prawns (shrimp) to the pan and cook for a further 1 minute or until the fish and prawns (shrimp) are just cooked. Remove from the flavoured stock with a slotted spoon and keep warm.

4 ▼ Heat the oil in a heavy-based pan or wok. Add the curry paste and cook for 1 minute. Stir in the coconut milk or cream, fish sauce, brown sugar, chillies and lime leaves.

5 Add the pineapple and cook until just heated through. Add the cooked fish and mix gently to combine.

6 Spoon into the reserved pineapple shells, if liked, and serve immediately, garnished with coriander (cilantro).

SESAME SALMON & CREAM SAUCE

Salmon fillet holds its shape when tossed in sesame seeds and stir-fried. It is served in a creamy turmeric sauce of diced courgettes (zucchini).

SERVES 4

INGREDIENTS:
625–750 g/1¼–1½ lb salmon or pink
    trout fillets
2 tbsp light soy sauce
3 tbsp sesame seeds
3 tbsp sunflower oil
4 spring onions (scallions), thinly sliced
    diagonally
2 large courgettes (zucchini), diced, or
    2.5 cm/5 inch piece of cucumber,
    diced
grated rind of ½ lemon
½ tsp turmeric
1 tbsp lemon juice
6 tbsp fish stock or water
3 tbsp double (heavy) cream or
    fromage frais
salt and pepper
frisée (chicory), to garnish (optional)

1 ▼ Skin the salmon and cut into strips about 4 × 2 cm/1½ × ¾ inches. Pat dry on paper towels. Season lightly, then brush with soy sauce and sprinkle all over with sesame seeds.

2 Heat 2 tablespoons of oil in the wok, swirling it around until really hot.

3 Add the pieces of salmon and stir-fry for 3–4 minutes until lightly browned all over. Remove with a fish slice, drain on paper towels and keep warm.

4 ▼ Add the remaining oil to the wok and when hot add the spring onions (scallions) and courgettes (zucchini) or cucumber and stir-fry for 1–2 minutes. Add the lemon rind and juice, turmeric, stock and seasoning and bring the mixture to the boil for a minute or so. Stir the cream or fromage frais into the sauce.

5 ▲ Return the salmon pieces to the wok and toss gently in the sauce until they are really hot. Serve on warm plates and garnish with frisée (chicory), if using.

WRAPPED FISH WITH GINGER BUTTER

This is fish cooked in a healthy, palate-tingling way. Whole mackerel or trout are stuffed with herbs, wrapped in foil or, more authentically, banana leaves, baked and then drizzled with a fresh ginger butter.

SERVES 4

INGREDIENTS:

4 x 250 g/8 oz whole trout or mackerel, gutted
4 tbsp chopped fresh coriander (cilantro)
5 garlic cloves, crushed
2 tsp grated lemon or lime zest
2 tsp vegetable oil
banana leaves, for wrapping (optional)
90 g/3 oz/6 tbsp butter
1 tbsp grated ginger root
1 tbsp light soy sauce
salt and pepper

TO GARNISH:

sprigs of fresh coriander (cilantro)
lemon or lime wedges

1 ▼ Wash and dry the fish. Mix the coriander (cilantro) with the garlic, lemon or lime zest and salt and pepper to taste. Spoon into the fish cavities.

2 Brush each fish with a little oil and season well with salt and pepper.

3 ▼ Place each fish on a double thickness of baking parchment or foil and wrap up well to enclose. Alternatively, wrap in banana leaves.

4 ▼ Place on a baking sheet and bake in a preheated oven at 190°C/375°F/ Gas Mark 5 for about 25 minutes or until the flesh will flake easily.

5 Meanwhile, melt the butter in a small pan. Add the grated ginger and stir until well mixed, then stir in the soy sauce.

6 To serve, unwrap the fish parcels, drizzle over the ginger butter and garnish with coriander (cilantro) and lemon or lime wedges.

FISH IN SZECHUAN HOT SAUCE

This is a classic Szechuan recipe. When served in a restaurant, the fish head and tail are removed before cooking.

SERVES 4

INGREDIENTS:

1 carp, bream, sea bass, trout, grouper or grey mullet, about 750g/1½ lb, gutted
1 tbsp light soy sauce
1 tbsp Chinese rice wine or dry sherry
vegetable oil, for deep-frying
sprigs of flat-leaf parsley or coriander (cilantro), to garnish

SAUCE:

2 garlic cloves, finely chopped
2–3 spring onions (scallions), finely chopped
1 tsp finely chopped ginger root
2 tbsp chilli bean sauce
1 tbsp tomato purée (paste)
2 tsp sugar
1 tbsp rice vingar
125 ml/4 fl oz/½ cup Chinese Stock (see page 10) or water
1 tbsp cornflour (cornstarch) paste (see page 15)
½ tsp sesame oil

1 ▼ Wash the fish and dry well on paper towels. Score both sides of the fish to the bone with a sharp knife, making diagonal cuts at intervals of about 2.5 cm/1 inch. Rub the fish with the soy sauce and rice wine on both sides, then leave on a plate in the refrigerator for 10–15 minutes.

2 Heat the oil in a preheated wok until smoking, to a temperature of 180–190°C/350–375°F. Deep-fry the fish for about 3–4 minutes on both sides, or until golden brown.

3 ▲ Pour off the oil, leaving about 1 tablespoon in the wok. Push the fish to one side of the wok and add the garlic, white parts of the spring onions (scallions), ginger, chilli bean sauce, tomato purée (paste), sugar, vinegar and stock. Bring to the boil and braise the fish in the sauce for 4–5 minutes, turning it over once.

4 ▼ Add the green parts of the spring onions (scallions) and stir in the cornflour (cornstarch) paste to thicken the sauce. Sprinkle with sesame oil and serve immediately, garnished with parsley or coriander (cilantro).

THAI PRAWN (SHRIMP) STIR-FRY

A very quick and tasty stir-fry using prawns (shrimp) and cucumber, cooked with the traditional flavourings of Thai cuisine – lemon grass, chilli and ginger.

SERVES 4

INGREDIENTS:
½ cucumber
2 tbsp sunflower oil
6 spring onions (scallions), halved lengthways and cut into 4 cm/1½ inch lengths
1 stalk lemon grass, sliced thinly
1 garlic clove, chopped
1 tsp chopped fresh red chilli
125 g/4 oz oyster mushrooms
1 tsp chopped ginger root
350 g/12 oz cooked peeled prawns (shrimp)
2 tsp cornflour (cornstarch)
2 tbsp water
1 tbsp dark soy sauce
½ tsp Thai fish sauce
2 tbsp Chinese rice wine or dry sherry
plain boiled rice, to serve

1 Cut the cucumber into strips about 5 mm × 4 cm/¼ × 1¾ inches.

2 ▼ Heat the sunflower oil in a wok or large frying pan (skillet), add the spring onions (scallions), cucumber strips, lemon grass, garlic, chilli, oyster mushrooms and ginger and stir-fry for 2 minutes.

3 ▼ Add the prawns (shrimp) and stir-fry for a further minute.

4 Mix together the cornflour (cornstarch), water, soy sauce and fish sauce until smooth.

5 ▼ Stir the cornflour (cornstarch) mixture and rice wine or sherry into the wok or pan (skillet) and heat through, stirring, until the sauce has thickened. Serve immediately with boiled rice.

SIZZLED CHILLI PRAWNS (SHRIMP)

Another Thai classic – large prawns (shrimp) marinated in a chilli mixture then stir-fried with cashews. Serve with fluffy rice and braised vegetables.

SERVES 4

INGREDIENTS:

5 tbsp soy sauce
5 tbsp dry sherry
3 dried red chillies, deseeded and chopped
2 garlic cloves, crushed
2 tsp grated ginger root
5 tbsp water
625 g/1¼ lb shelled tiger prawns (shrimp)
1 large bunch spring onions (scallions), chopped
90 g/3 oz/⅔ cup salted cashew nuts
3 tbsp vegetable oil
2 tsp cornflour (cornstarch)

1 ▼ Mix the soy sauce with the sherry, chillies, garlic, ginger and water in a large bowl.

2 Add the prawns (shrimp), spring onions (scallions) and cashews and mix well. Cover tightly and leave to marinate for at least 2 hours, stirring occasionally.

3 ▲ Heat the oil in a large, heavy-based frying pan (skillet) or wok. Drain the prawns (shrimp), spring onions (scallions) and cashews from the marinade with a slotted spoon and add to the pan, reserving the marinade. Stir-fry over a high heat for 1–2 minutes.

4 ▲ Mix the reserved marinade with the cornflour (cornstarch), add to the pan and stir-fry for about 30 seconds, until the marinade forms a slightly thickened shiny glaze over the prawn (shrimp) mixture. Serve immediately with rice.

STIR-FRIED PRAWNS (SHRIMP)

This colourful and delicious dish is cooked with vegetables: vary them according to seasonal availability.

SERVES 4

INGREDIENTS:
60 g/2 oz mangetout (snow peas)
½ small carrot, thinly sliced
60 g/2 oz baby sweetcorn
60 g/2 oz straw mushrooms
175–250 g/6–8 oz raw tiger prawns (shrimp), peeled
pinch of salt
½ egg white, lightly beaten
1 tsp cornflour (cornstarch) paste (see page 15)
about 300ml/½ pint/1¼ cups vegetable oil
1 spring onion (scallion), cut into short pieces
4 slices ginger root, peeled and finely chopped
½ tsp sugar
1 tbsp light soy sauce
1 tsp Chinese rice wine or dry sherry
few drops of sesame oil

1 Top and tail the mangetout (snow peas). Cut the carrot into the same size as the mangetout (snow peas). Halve the baby sweetcorn and straw mushrooms.

2 ▲ Mix the prawns (shrimp) with a pinch of salt, the egg white and cornflour (cornstarch) paste.

3 ▼ Heat a wok over a high heat for 2–3 minutes, then add the oil and heat to medium hot before adding the prawns (shrimp); stir to separate them. Remove with a slotted spoon as soon as the colour changes.

4 ▼ Pour off the oil, leaving about 1 tablespoon in the wok. Add all the vegetables and stir-fry for about 1 minute. Add the prawns (shrimp) and the seasonings. Blend well. Sprinkle with sesame oil and serve hot.

SZECHUAN PRAWNS (SHRIMP)

Raw prawns (shrimp) should be used if possible, otherwise omit steps 1 and 2 and add the ready-cooked prawns (shrimp) before the sauce ingredients at the beginning of step 3.

SERVES 4

INGREDIENTS:
250–300 g/8–10 oz raw tiger prawns (shrimp)
pinch of salt
¼ egg white, lightly beaten
1 tsp cornflour (cornstarch) paste (see page 15)
600 ml/1 pint/2¼ cups vegetable oil
fresh coriander (cilantro) leaves, to garnish

SAUCE:
1 tsp finely chopped ginger root
2 spring onions (scallions), finely chopped
1 garlic clove, finely chopped
3–4 small dried red chillies, deseeded and chopped
1 tbsp light soy sauce
1 tsp Chinese rice wine or dry sherry
1 tbsp tomato purée (paste)
1 tbsp oyster sauce
2–3 tbsp Chinese Stock (see page 10) or water
few drops of sesame oil

1 ▲ Peel the raw prawns (shrimp), then mix with the salt, egg white and cornflour (cornstarch) paste until well coated.

2 ▼ Heat the oil in a preheated wok until it is smoking, at a temperature of 180–190°C/350–375°F. Deep-fry the prawns (shrimp) in the hot oil for about 1 minute. Remove with a slotted spoon and drain on paper towels.

3 Pour off the oil, leaving about 1 tablespoon in the wok.

4 ▼ Add all the ingredients for the sauce to the wok, bring the sauce mixture to the boil and stir until smooth and well blended.

5 Add the prawns (shrimp) to the sauce and stir until blended well. Serve garnished with coriander (cilantro) leaves.

FRIED SQUID FLOWERS

The addition of green (bell) pepper and black bean sauce to the squid makes a colourful and delicious dish.

SERVES 4

❀❀❀❀❀❀❀❀❀❀❀❀❀❀❀❀❀❀❀

INGREDIENTS:
*350–400 g/12–14 oz prepared and
   cleaned squid (see page 38)
1 medium green (bell) pepper, cored
   and deseeded
3–4 tbsp vegetable oil
1 garlic clove, finely chopped
¼ tsp finely chopped ginger root
2 tsp finely chopped spring onions
   (scallions)
¼ tsp salt
2 tbsp crushed black bean sauce
1 tsp Chinese rice wine or dry sherry
few drops of sesame oil*

❀❀❀❀❀❀❀❀❀❀❀❀❀❀❀❀❀❀❀

1 ▲ Open up the squid and score in a criss-cross pattern. Cut into pieces the size of an oblong postage stamp.

2 ▲ Blanch in a bowl of boiling water for a few seconds. Remove and drain; dry well on paper towels.

3 ▲ Cut the (bell) pepper into small triangular pieces. Heat the oil in a preheated wok, or a heavy-based frying pan (skillet), and stir-fry the (bell) pepper for about 1 minute. Add the garlic, ginger, spring onion (scallion), salt and squid. Continue stirring for another minute.

4 ▲ Finally add the black bean sauce and rice wine or sherry, and blend well. Serve hot, sprinkled with drops of sesame oil.

SPICED SCALLOPS

Scallops are available both fresh and frozen. Make sure they are completely defrosted before cooking.

SERVES 4

INGREDIENTS:
*12 large scallops with corals (roe)
  attached, defrosted if frozen, or
  350 g/12 oz small scallops without
  corals (roe), defrosted*
4 tbsp sunflower oil
*4–6 spring onions (scallions), thinly
  sliced diagonally*
1 garlic clove, crushed
*2.5 cm/1 inch ginger root, finely
  chopped*
250 g/8 oz mangetout (snow peas)
*125 g/4 oz button or closed-cup
  mushrooms, sliced*
2 tbsp sherry
2 tbsp soy sauce
1 tbsp clear honey
¼ tsp ground allspice
salt and pepper
1 tbsp sesame seeds, toasted

1 Wash and dry the scallops, discarding any black pieces and detach the corals (roe), if using. Slice each scallop into 3–4 pieces and if the corals are large halve them.

2 ▲ Heat 2 tablespoons of oil in the wok, swirling it around until really hot. Add the spring onions (scallions), garlic and ginger and stir-fry for a minute or so, then add the mangetout (snow peas) and continue to cook for 2–3 minutes, stirring continuously. Remove to a bowl.

3 ▼ Add the remaining oil to the wok. When it is really hot, add the scallops and corals (roe) and stir-fry for a couple of minutes. Add the mushrooms and continue to cook for a further minute or so.

4 ▼ Add the sherry, soy sauce, honey and allspice to the wok, with salt and pepper to taste. Mix thoroughly, then return the mangetout (snow peas) mixture to the wok.

5 Season well and toss together over a high heat for a minute or so until piping hot. Serve immediately, sprinkled with sesame seeds.

INDEX